The Bonhoeffer Legacy: Australasian Journal of Bonhoeffer Studies

ATF Theology
Adelaide

2014

The Bonhoeffer Legacy: Australasian Journal of Bonhoeffer Studies
Volume 2, Issue 1, 2014

The Bonhoeffer Legacy: Australasian Journal of Bonhoeffer Studies is a fully refereed academic journal aimed principally at providing an outlet for an ever expanding Bonhoeffer scholarship in Australia, New Zealand and the South Pacific region, as well as being open to article submissions from Bonhoeffer scholars throughout the world. It also aims to elicit and encourage future and ongoing scholarship in the field. The focus of the journal, captured in the notion of 'Legacy', is on any aspect of Bonhoeffer's life, theology and political action that is relevant to his immense contribution to twentieth century events and scholarship. 'Legacy' can be understood as including those events and ideas that contributed to Bonhoeffer's own development, those that constituted his own context or those that have developed since his time as a result of his work. The editors encourage and welcome any scholarship that contributes to the journal's aims. The journal also has book reviews.

Subscription rates 2014

Print	Online	Print and online
Aus $65	Aus $55 individuals	Aus $75 individuals
Aus $90 institutions	$80 institutions	Aus $100 institutions

The Bonhoeffer Legacy: Australasian Journal of Bonhoeffer Studies is published by ATF Theology and imprint of ATF (Australia) Ltd (ABN 90 116 359 963) and is published once a year.
ISSN 2202-9168

 www.atfpress.com

Vol 2/ 1 2014

Table of Contents

Contributors

Dr Keith Clements is a former Lecturer at Bristol University, UK and former General Secretary of the Conference of European Churches, Geneva, Switzerland.

Dallas Gingles is completing a doctorate on Bonhoefferian theology at Southern Methodist University, Dallas, Texas, USA.

Dr Christopher Holmes is a Senior Lecturer in Theology at the University of Otago, Dunedin, New Zealand.

Professor Terence Lovat is Emeritus Professor at the University of Newcastle, Australia, and Senior Research Fellow at Oxford University, UK.

Dr Derek McDougall is Principal Fellow at the University of Melbourne, Australia.

Dr Joseph McGarry is a Lecturer in Divinity at the University of Aberdeen, Scotland, UK.

Dianne Rayson is completing a doctorate with a Flechtheim scholoraship on Bonhoefferian theology at the University of Newcastle, NSW, Australia.

Dr Maurice Schild is a former Lecturer at the Lutheran Theological College, University of Divinity, Adelaide, Australia.

Dr WG Watson was formerly Head of Systematic Theology Trinity College, Brisbane.

Vol 2/ 1 2014

Editorial

The Bonhoeffer Legacy: Australasian Journal of Bonhoeffer Studies is aimed principally at providing an outlet for an ever expanding Bonhoeffer scholarship in Australia, New Zealand and the South Pacific region. It also aims to elicit and encourage future and ongoing scholarship in the field. The focus of the journal, captured in the notion of 'Legacy', is on any aspect of Bonhoeffer's life, theology and political action that is relevant to his immense contribution to twentieth and twenty-first century events and scholarship. 'Legacy' can be understood as including those events and ideas that contributed to Bonhoeffer's own development, those that constituted his own context or those that have developed since his time as a result of his work. In other words, Bonhoeffer's legacy can be traced back to the many events, philosophies and theologies that preceded his time as well as drawn forward to help in understanding the world we inhabit today, especially around issues of faith, non-faith and the ethics entailed in human action.

In this first issue of the second volume, we include some members of the international Bonhoeffer community, as well as established and newer members of the Australasian community. Again, the tapestry of issues covered is illustrative of the richness and diversity of Bonhoefferian theology. Perhaps partly because of the untimely ending of his life, his work is the equivalent of the unfinished symphony, a veritable unfinished theology that therefore leaves much space for exploration by those of us who come after. As well as and partly because of the richness, diversity and unfinished nature of it, his theology presents as an open canvas on which to sketch and explore theological issues past, present and future. These articles capture something of this multi-directionality.

In the first article, Christopher Holmes from Otago University, New Zealand, writes on the theme of resurrection and reality in Bonhoeffer's theology. In the second article, Joseph McGarry of the University of Aberdeen, Scotland, writes on the influence of Bonhoeffer's early theology on his main work on *Discipleship*. Dallas Gingles of Southern Methodist University, Texas, USA, writes next on Bonhoeffer's ethics of responsibility as a qualified virtue ethics. In the fourth article, Maurice Schild of the University of Divinity, Adelaide, Australia, recovers an earlier article from the *Lutheran Theological Journal* that compares and contrast Bonhoeffer with his contemporary, Hermann Sasse. In the final research article, Dianne Rayson and Terence Lovat of the University of Newcastle, NSW, Australia, explore Bonhoeffer's Christology and his interest in the Indian religious traditions in searching for the foundations for a contemporary eco-theological ethics. A special entry in this issue is a copy of the speech given by Keith Clements, a doyen of Bonhoeffer scholarship, at the 2013 International Bonhoeffer Society banquet.

As can be seen in the above array of contributions, Bonhoeffer's theology truly is an unfinished one with an unusual capacity to be taken in any direction and to serve multiple purposes. In each case, the articles convey the distinctiveness of what this journal describes as 'the Bonhoeffer Legacy'.

Terence Lovat
Newcastle, Australia
July, 2014

Vol 2/ 1 2014

Resurrection and Reality in the Theology of Dietrich Bonhoeffer

Christopher RJ Holmes

Introduction

Dietrich Bonhoeffer has a rather profound understanding of the Gospel. What renders it profound is its steadfast yielding to a particular person. That person is of course Jesus Christ, crucified and risen. For Bonhoeffer, Jesus Christ is neither an idea nor a symbol, one who instantiates something greater than himself, for example justice, of which he may be said to be an exemplar of sorts. Rather, Jesus Christ is a living person who as such is present. His presence is precisely what generates statements about his identity as true God and true human. In other words, that we can and do ask questions about *who* he is, is a function of his presence, his contemporaneity in relationship to us.[1] Bonhoeffer's theology, often with a dazzling degree of success, points to the one thing that above all else must be minded as the one thing, that one thing being the living Lord Jesus Christ and all things in relationship to him.

'Living'

The word 'living' is crucial to consider. Most of the time it would seem that Jesus Christ is dead and gone. If the church considers Jesus Christ at all, it is most often as one who is imprisoned by the past, one who must be unlocked and freed by our own efforts. Should we want to speak of him, many self-described Christian people think that we must endeavor to make him relevant, to provide some kind bridge as

---

1. For a classical account of this theme, see Hans W Frei, *The Identity of Jesus Christ: The Hermeneutical Bases of Dogmatic Theology* (Eugene, OR: Wipf and Stock, 1997).

it were whereby he can be made intelligible to the people and world of late modern global capitalism. Such efforts are for Bonhoeffer misguided and doomed to fail. In this article I offer an account of why Bonhoeffer thinks they are doomed to fail, and what the Christian community might learn from their impending failure.

Efforts to make Christ relevant fail because they do not appreciate the extent to which the 'historical is that which is here and now'.[2] This is Bonhoeffer's question: How can it be that a seemingly past actor and event be now present and on the scene? The answer is simply because of the 'empty grave'.[3] Bonhoeffer refers to the empty grave as 'one of the most decisive elements of Christology'.[4] In this article I take up Bonhoeffer's account of the resurrection of Jesus Christ is his Christology Lectures of 1933. I will ask what the event of the resurrection teaches us in response to the question—'Who do you say that I am?'[5] Furthermore, in asking what the resurrection teaches us about who Christ is, I will also ask about the relationship between Christ's resurrection and reality. This is only fitting given that the language of 'reality' occupies a prominent place in Bonhoeffer's *Ethics* manuscripts. Bonhoeffer uses the word 'reality' not only to describe what Christ does, that is bring about the real world, but also to describe who he is, someone who is *reality* itself. There is, I think, a more than tangential relationship between the two. In this piece, I unfold something of what that relationship might be said to be. The resurrected Jesus is not only reality; he also brings reality—the reality he is—into being. Put differently, Christ is, as Bonhoeffer argues, the subject and agent of reality.

I undertake this brief exploration with a particular end in mind. That end is the promotion of an account of Bonhoeffer as a doctrinal theologian. Although I have quite serious reservations about certain doctrinal dimensions of Bonhoeffer's theology, especially in regards to theology proper, I continue not only as a professional theologian but also as one ordained to the ministry of Word and sacrament

---

2. Dietrich Bonhoeffer Works, edited by Victoria J Barnett and Barbara Wojhoski, 'Lectures on Christology', in *Berlin: 1932–1933,* volume 12, edited Larry L Rasmussen (Minneapolis: Fortress Press, 2009), 330 (hereafter *DBWE*).
3. *DBWE,* volume 12, 359.
4. *DBWE,* volume 12, 359.
5. Matt 16:14.

to read him, always finding myself enriched in the process as I am brought face to face with the living Christ, the Christ who is his Gospel.[6] This article will have succeeded to the extent that it reminds us that Bonhoeffer's enduring contribution to the life of the Christian community is the extent to which his Lectures on Christology and his *Ethics* facilitate with piercing insight encounter in relation to the whole counsel of Christ.

Christology Lectures

I will structure my treatment of Bonhoeffer's Christology Lectures by examining a few key statements he makes about the resurrection. First, Bonhoeffer is convinced, rightly so, that the Jesus of history/ Christ of faith distinction is unhelpful.[7] The Jesus of history is the Christ of faith. He lies neither behind nor in front of the biblical text but speaks through it, creating by the Holy Spirit the faith to receive him as the one who discloses himself there. Similarly, Bonhoeffer

---

6. For an account of these reservations, see my piece 'Eberhard Jüngel's Soteriologically Minded Doctrine of the Trinity: Some Commendations and Reservations', in *Indicative of Grace—Imperative of Freedom: Essays in Honour of Eberhard Jüngel*, edited by R Derek Nelson (London: T&T Clark, 2014).

7. Note that the lack of a distinction is not to suggest that Bonhoeffer is disrespectful of Bultmann. This is a topic productively opened up in Gerhard Krause's essay 'Dietrich Bonhoeffer and Rudolf Bultmann', in *The Future of our Religious Past: Essays in Honour of Rudolph Bultmann*, edited by James M Robinson (London: SCM, 1971). Krause writes, 'Bonhoeffer sketches his demand for a non-religious interpretation of biblical concepts in pointed discussion with Bultmann's project for demythologizing, and he sees an affinity between them as over against all other theological programmes'. (304). See also Bonhoeffer's letters to Eberhard Bethge of May 5 and June 8, 1944. Bonhoeffer writes, 'My opinion of it [Bultmann's essay of 1941, 'New Testament and Mythology'] today would be that he went not "too far," as most people thought, but rather not far enough. It's not only "mythological" concepts like miracles, ascension, and so one (which in principle can't be separated from concepts of God, faith, etc.!) that are problematic, but "religious" concepts as such. You can't separate God from the miracles (as Bultmann things); instead, you must be able to interpret and proclaim them *both* "non-religiously". (May 5) Put somewhat differently, Bonhoeffer writes in the later letter, 'My view, however, is that the full content, including the 'mythological' concepts, must remain—the New Testament is not a mythological dressing up of a universal truth, but this mythology (resurrection and so forth) is the thing itself!—but that these concepts must not be interpreted in a way that does not make religion the condition for faith.' *DBWE*, volume 8, *Letters and Papers from Prison*, 372, 430.

is no friend of Lessing's ugly ditch—'accidental truths of history can never become the proof of necessary truths of reason'.[8] Indeed, "access to the historical Jesus," Bonhoeffer writes, 'is only made possible by Jesus' resurrection'.[9] The way to speak of this particular historical person, Jesus of Nazareth, is to speak of him as resurrected. The risen Jesus creates his faith in us in such a way that we are enabled to access his history as contemporaneous with our own. This is a key move. The only Jesus the New Testament witnesses would have us attest is the risen One. He speaks today, and just so he meets us through the pages of Holy Scripture. But the Christ who is risen, who speaks through Scripture, the Christ who is *for us* is, Bonhoeffer avers, a historical figure. We encounter the resurrected and exalted Christ as the crucified one. The one who encounters us through the sacred page is the same Christ who told Peter, on shores of Galilee, to 'follow me!'[10] Because he was raised, Jesus obliterates the difference— again, Lessing's gap—between the 'then and there' and the 'here and now'. To put it in more technical terms, the resurrection is not only epistemologically primary but ontologically primary as well. It is epistemologically primary insofar as the only Jesus one can know is the risen Jesus—the rest are idols. The resurrection is ontologically primary because, as Bonhoeffer says, the 'historical comes from God's eternity'.[11] By way of explanation, that is to say that the Jew Jesus, the man from Nazareth, born of the virgin Mary, is also one eternally born of the Father, born in time and of eternity. The resurrection does not establish him as *God from God, light from light* but rather confirms what has always been the case, namely that this man is God's Son, begotten and not made.

Some of this might sound rather too realized, too accomplished, lacking a kind of eschatological horizon if you will. If such a reservation sounds about right, Bonhoeffer has already anticipated your worries. The resurrected and exalted Jesus is one who can only be received as the crucified one. Bonhoeffer insists that the resurrection does not

---

8. Gotthold Lessing, *Lessing's Theological Writings,* translated by Henry Chadwick (London: Black, 1956), 53.
9. *DBWE*, volume 12, 330.
10. John 21:23.
11. *DBWE*, volume 12, 331.

obviate the 'stumbling block', the stumbling block that is the cross.[12] Rather, the resurrection intensifies it. Jesus, Bonhoeffer argues, 'does not emerge from his incognito, not even as the Risen One'.[13] Not until Jesus comes again will he be revealed as the One he is, the very centre of the new creation that comes into being in a proleptic sense in his death and resurrection. Cross and resurrection are therefore moments of the Christ event that are profoundly intertwined. As the resurrected one Jesus bears his wounds, the marks of his crucifixion. The 'No' of Jesus' own people and the collusion of the Gentiles in that 'No' remains forever etched into him. The "God-human" who bears our sins, our 'No', has, however, forever absorbed the marks of our 'No' into his person, triumphing over them.[14] In his person he brings a new world into being, a world shorn of sin and death. He is the new creation.

Bonhoeffer asks, 'With what reality will we reckon in our life?. . . with the resurrection or with death?'[15] There is reality *and* there is reality, for Bonhoeffer; the pseudo reality that is death is false and bankrupt, even though it comports itself as if it were alive. That is just how mischievous this pseudo-reality is. There is another reality, and that reality 'is the reality of God that is revealed in Jesus Christ'.[16] Reality, for Bonhoeffer, is not what you make of it. Rather, it is something that is alive, that is received, the content of which lies entirely *extra nos*. Reality is, in other words, revealed, radically given in Jesus Christ. In Jesus Christ we 'are placed before the reality of a reconciled world'.[17] The Christology Lectures and the *Ethics* manuscripts are most deeply united at just this point. Christ is the turning point, the decisive marker of the end of the old age, the age of sin and death; he not only announces the new age, the new age of holiness and peace in him, but brings it about in his person. The reconciliation he accomplishes in his person by suffering our NO, by existing in the likeness of sinful flesh, makes the world new. It is *reality*. That we believe or disbelieve makes no difference at this point. Our subjective disposition towards

---

12. *DBWE*, volume 12, 359.
13. *DBWE*, volume 12, 360.
14. *DBWE*, volume 12, 356.
15. *DBWE*, 'Christ, Reality, and Good', in DBWE, volume 6, edited by Clifford J Green, 49.
16. *DBWE*, volume 6, 49.
17. *DBWE*, volume 6, 73.

what Christ achieves in his person neither verifies it nor falsifies it. The world is indeed reconciled. It is to the reconciliation that is Jesus Christ that the Christian community gives witness.

Christian existence is existence that lives 'before the reality of a reconciled world'.[18] It is existence that lives in and from the second Adam. Bonhoeffer's instincts are deeply Pauline on this point, as in so many others. Romans 5:12–21 is one of his canons within the canon. Indeed, Bonhoeffer notes that 'what happened to Christ has happened for all, for he was *the* human being. The new human being has been created'.[19] In Jesus Christ the old Adam has passed away; he has been crucified. But more than that, a new human being has been made. You see, Bonhoeffer cannot conceive of humankind (Jews and Gentiles) apart from Jesus Christ. Christ is the substitute and representative of all precisely as the true Israelite in whom there is no fault. He is the 'human being accepted, judged, and awakened by God to a new life'.[20] The resurrection has, for Bonhoeffer, this crucial payoff, namely that it creates a new human being, mortifies the old and vivifies in accord with the new. To conceive of oneself truly is therefore to conceive of oneself and indeed the cosmos in Christ. Christ is one's true self— think Galatians 2:20. The resurrection is the new and hidden centre of humanity's existence. It is not only revelatory of God' s salutary 'No' to our sin but the power and form of a new life. Christian life, which is but new life, is resurrection life.

The miracle of the resurrection of which the empty tomb is the 'visible authentication' overturns the 'idolization of death'.[21] Our idolization of death—past and present—is, thanks be to the God and Father of our Lord Jesus Christ, broken by the miracle of the resurrection. Late modern people living in an age of global capitalistic consumption are people who are anxious precisely because they demand 'eternities from life'.[22] The resurrection of Christ frees us from demanding 'eternities from life'.[23] This is because with the risen One a new humanity has been born from whom 'proceeds all the

---

18. *DBWE*, volume 6, 73.
19. 'Ethics as Formation', in *DBWE*, volume 6, 91.
20. *DBWE*, volume 6, 92.
21. *DBWE*, volume 12, 359; *DBWE*, volume 6, 91.
22. *DBWE*, volume 6, 92.
23. *DBWE*, volume 6, 92.

formation of a world reconciled with God'.[24] We idolise death and thus resist the proclamation of the resurrected one because we are obsessed with autonomy, with having it our own way. We despise the way of particularity, which is the way of the cross, the way that teaches us to follow him who puts to death all that is in accord with the old and frees us for the life that is truly life, which is the life of obedience. Were Christ not raised, Bonhoeffer seems to be saying, there would be nothing to stop us from worshipping what kills us, namely death, and so nothing that would prevent us from falling into and succumbing to the abyss of nothingness.

We become human inasmuch as we participate in the resurrection which is 'the renewal of human being'.[25] The resurrection is the true form of human being, our true form being Christ. The resurrection is the renewal of our humanity, indeed of all humanity, the humanity that Christ takes on and judges through his cross. To take the resurrection seriously is to live in light of this renewal, to live as if Christ were 'one's own true nature'.[26] In an age that would have us privatize or worse abscond from the particularity of Christ, Bonhoeffer reminds us that our trying to make ourselves is entirely futile. Rather, we become a 'self' inasmuch as we put on Christ as our own true nature in confirmation of our baptism in him. In words that are strong and quite difficult for us to hear, Bonhoeffer writes that 'Christ's cross is the death sentence on the world'.[27] The world that he is talking about is of course the world put to death in Jesus' death, that is the world of the old Adam. The content of faith, for Bonhoeffer, is Christ. My faith—your faith—does not save. No, Christ's faith saves; he puts to death our faith in false gods, most especially ourselves. His faithfulness onto death makes the world new, and gives us the power to live in accord with that newness. To be a true self is, therefore, to be found in him.

There is just so much good news in all of this. The reality that the 'God-human' is raised makes 'an end of death and calls a new creation into life. God gives new life'.[28] Death dies, and new creation

---

24. *DBWE*, volume 6, 92.
25. 'Guilt, Justification, and Renewal', in *DBWE*, volume 6, 134.
26. *DBWE*, volume 6, 134.
27. 'Ultimate and Penultimate Things', in *DBWE*, volume 6, 158.
28. *DBWE*, volume 6, 158.

arises in and through this particular person. Accordingly, God is not interested in abolishing the world but rather of ending the world that is incongruent with his covenantal purposes. The world that ends is the world of the old Adam. The world that begins is a world that has a future and a hope, both of which are a living reality in Jesus Christ. Note again the language of living. Reality is not a set of propositions, an idea, a symbol; it is, instead, a person, a living person who not only brings about the new creation but is its very reality and form.

Bonhoeffer does not so emphasise death's death in Christ that little remains to be said about the form of new life that it evokes and the kind of creaturely response it generates. The new life—which is the life of Christ—'creates space for itself in earthly life'.[29] This is a crucial point to reflect on. Far from downplaying the significance of the 'penultimate', that is earthly life, Bonhoeffer, by so emphasising Christ's resurrection, invests earthly life with a new sense of dignity and urgency. Life in Christ is worldly life, meaning that it demands our full participation in earthly life. 'New life', says Bonhoeffer, '*creates space for itself in earthly life*.'[30] The penultimate is not a stepping-stone toward the ultimate, understood as some kind of disembodied heavenly life. By no means: earthly life is to be rendered transparent to the ultimate, which is Jesus Christ. The risen Jesus takes up space on earth, and he does so through his body, the church, so as to create a community that heralds and anticipates in its words and deeds the life to come. The church is the first-fruits of Christ's resurrected life. Thus life in Christ is ecclesial life. This is not life that absconds from the earthly. Human life is life lived in Christ and for Christ in the here and now. Christ humanises us, makes us more, rather than less, human. We are made human 'in a new resurrection way that is completely unlike the old'.[31] The old is characterized by death. It is offended by Christ and will stop at nothing to silence him, even to the point of crucifying him; whereas the new life is lived in Christ for the sake of the world he loves, and strives to yield to Christ by the power of his Spirit at every point.

The resurrection of Jesus Christ from the dead does fundamental theological work for Bonhoeffer. The resurrection attests the

---

29. *DBWE*, volume 6, 158.
30. *DBWE*, volume 6, 158.
31. *DBWE*, volume 6, 158.

fundamental truth that the 'disunion of human beings from God has been overcome'.[32] The Christian community, following Jesus Christ himself, is to speak as if it (disunion) has been overcome in him, comport itself as such, as indeed such disunion has been overcome. The resurrection of Christ from the dead is reality, to be sure; and, astonishingly, it is making itself real, felt as it were in the church which suffers the cruciform form of his presence. Accordingly, Christ's presence cannot be domesticated but can only be attested in the lives of those who attest the most basic truth of all, namely that disunion has been overcome (and is being overcome) in the Spirit, union with God itself being the 'new norm' to which we are to be conformed.

To sum up this section, then: Bonhoeffer's Lectures of 1933 would have us ask the right question of Jesus Christ, that is 'Who are you?'[33] That we can even ask the right question is because Christ is present to us, speaking through his scriptural Word. He would have us not try to answer the 'Who' question for ourselves but rather with open hands hear him as he interprets himself to us. To speak faithfully of Jesus Christ is to listen, and thus to allow all of one's preconceived ideas about him to dissipate as he himself speaks through Scripture. If we hear him speak with the ears he gives us to hear by his Spirit, we come to learn that he is a living reality, indeed *the* living reality and so our reality, too. The resurrection is the moment upon which the Christ event turns, the announcement and vindication of the claim that this one is truly the 'God-human', and that life is found *in* him.

Further to this, we noted that the centrality of the resurrection for Bonhoeffer's description of Christ's person as a living person anticipates the language of reality as present throughout the *Ethics* manuscripts. The resurrected Christ is definitive, we noted, of reality. He is reality. What he achieves in his person—reconciliation—makes the world what it is, a reconciled world, and in the power of the Spirit he awakens women and men to live as if this were really true, which of course it is. Accordingly, the world is subject to this particular reconciling act of God which gives rise to the new humanity whose shape and form is Christ. The new reality is one that is shorn of the power of death, freed *from* the idolization of death, and in turn freed *for* new life with God. Given this, it is now appropriate, I think, to

---

32. 'God's Love and the Disintegration of the World', in *DBWE*, volume 6, 311.
33. *DBWE*, volume 12, 302.

step back and make a few remarks about the rich pastoral resources present in Bonhoeffer's account of the resurrected Christ as the basis and form of reality.

The Resurrected Christ as Reality

To be a pastor is to be continually engaged in the difficult and demanding work of re-contextualising disorder.[34] This is the work that the Gospel requires. The pastor in proclaiming the Gospel cares for the congregational soul. To care for the soul is to care for a soul that has—whether it really believes it or not—been awakened to and for new existence in the resurrected Jesus. Accordingly, the pastor understands their ministry to be that of encouraging people to live as those awakened to the life that is truly life, that is the obedient life of Jesus Christ. The pastor thus has a kind of prophetic responsibility. Inasmuch as she witnesses to the one who triumphed over death, she calls the people of God to forsake idols. Indeed, the pastor recognizes that human beings are incredibly adept at making idols. Through the proclamation of the Word and the right administration of the sacraments, she shares in Jesus' ongoing ministry of tearing down our idols and conforming us anew to him who is our true form.

The pastor, moreover, has confidence in what she preaches— Christ crucified—because of the crucified one's having been raised. Not only the pastor, but the entire Christian community, does not work at trying to make Jesus relevant to late modern consumers. Instead, the Christian community proclaims a Gospel that is real, one that does not need to be made real. This is a Gospel that is creating a people for itself, even if need be of calling forth stones to sing its praises. Why Bonhoeffer is worth wrestling with is because he gives us a Gospel that is relentlessly christocentric, and because of that one that inspires confidence. The resurrection of Jesus has unmasked and continues to unmask our idols. It does just that! It breaks the power of death, and in so doing renews human life. Bonhoeffer's Lectures on Christology and his *Ethics* manuscripts renew the church inasmuch as they remind it of the continue call to wrestle with reality, and

---

34. This insight is taken from Ray S Anderson. He argues that the church 'is responsible to know the difference between order and disorder, but wise enough to contextualize disorder with grace and truth'. See *On Being Human: Essays in Theological Anthropology* (Pasadena, CA: Fuller Seminary Press, 1982), 129.

indeed to be conformed to it. 'With what reality will we reckon in our life? With the reality of God's revelatory word or with the so-called realities of life? With divine grace or with earthly inadequacies? With the resurrection or with death?'[35]

Besides engaging in the ministry of recontextualisation, the pastoral office is rightly deemed a political office. There is nothing remotely apolitical in Bonhoeffer's Lectures or his *Ethics* manuscripts, especially in regards to the political nature of our discipleship. I use this term 'political' in quite a careful and qualified sense. I say this because the penultimate, the earthly, is subject to 'a going on', the first-fruits of which are Jesus' having been raised. He is the new creation come. The resurrection is the event that heralds the future which is already proleptically present even if only in the shape of a mustard seed, and even if only all too provisionally attested by the Christian community. This Christ event is of course political insofar as it reveals the ultimate reality, the one who reigns over all people and things.

Politics is a difficult term to locate in Bonhoeffer. Bonhoeffer's language of the 'penultimate' and 'ultimate' is helpful here inasmuch as the penultimate, which is the earthly realm, one of whose basic feature is the state, has a centre, and that centre is Christ.[36] The state, as is the case with the individual, aspires toward autonomy; to the extent that the state strives to be autonomous, it forfeits God's call for it to be that which administers justice, horizontally speaking. The state as a form of God's rule for restraining licentiousness, curbing violence, etc, can only be what it is called to be inasmuch as it recognizes that its intelligibility is extrinsic to itself. Its principle of intelligibility is Jesus Christ. He frees the state, as he does people, from idolizing death, from demanding eternities of itself. The state is thus to exercise its rule in the name of another, and to the extent that it does so, it fulfills its mandate, so Bonhoeffer argues.

Christ's conforming of all our life to the reality that he is, involves, as many of you will know, 'mandates'.[37] Christ wills to take form in the world through the mandates. Whether it be church, family, work, or government, the mandates fulfill their task inasmuch as they

---

35. 'Christ, Reality, and Good. Christ, Church, and World' in *DBWE*, volume 6, 49.
36. See 'Ultimate and Penultimate Things', in *DBWE*, volume 6; *DBWE*, volume 12, 325–27, wherein Bonhoeffer describes Christ as 'the Center of History'.
37. See 'The Concrete Commandment and the Divine Mandates', in *DBWE*, volume 6.

encourage us to be responsible for one another in the name of the one who has taken and takes responsibility for us. The pastor is called to witness (as are all God's people) to the fact that Christ wills to take form in the world through a people. Pastoral ministry is ministry in the name of Another, this Other who is reality. The church's witness is therefore profoundly political in nature inasmuch as it bears witness to Christ's work of making the mandates permeable and transparent to his will and presence.

Ministry is a highly charged political undertaking because it continues to put forth before the people of God the question which they are continually tempted to demur from answering. That question is, as alluded to a moment ago, a matter of sovereignty and of rulership over the earth. The response to the question is also a confession: Jesus is Lord of all. Bonhoeffer's theology offers us subtle and bold resources whereby we might live into and in light of this claim that Christ indeed rules the earth. The 'ruler of this world' of which John's Gospel speaks is a sham ruler: he has already been condemned.[38] Ministry is about bearing witness to the real ruler and in so doing trusting that the Spirit is at work awakening to new life.

Conclusion

In sum, the One who is resurrected is reality. The reconciliation he achieves in his person is what is real, and he is at work revealing it, calling a people forth in the service of his self-revelation. Christian existence is existence that corresponds to the One who is the hidden centre and who would have us live responsibly in relation to him. 'Our lives are hid with Christ in God', writes Paul.[39] It would be entirely appropriate to read Bonhoeffer's Christology Lectures and *Ethics* manuscripts as an extended commentary on that theme. The joy of Christian ministry and indeed of theology is to ask *who* is this One in whom are lives are hid? Is he the reality with which we will reckon? I would hope so. Bonhoeffer, as a disciple of Jesus Christ, would have us accept that our lives are hid in him, and so live as to give witness to our lives as being located in him.

---

38. John 12:31.
39. Col 3:3.

Vol 2/ 1 2014

Bridging the Gap:
Dietrich Bonhoeffer's Early Theology and its influence on *Discipleship*

Joseph McGarry

Introduction

In January 1961, Eberhard Bethge gave the Aldin Tuthill Lectures at Chicago Theological Seminary, under the title 'The Challenge of Dietrich Bonhoffer's Life and Theology'.[1] These lectures, still very er ·ly in the development of Bonhoeffer reception—particularly for the English speaking world—gave an overview of his life and thought. In specific, Bethge sought to demonstrate a broad continuity within Bonhoeffer's work, even as he acknowledged significant transitions and maturation along the way. Bethge urged his listeners to see Bonhoeffer as a theologian ahead of his time, rejecting talk of the orders of creation when they were coming into vogue in favor of 'an irritant eschatology'.[2] Then, when others later turned to eschatology, Bonhoeffer had already returned to the worldliness of Christian faith. Bethge's point was to demonstrate that Bonhoeffer's thought was always in transition, always maturing, and yet always progressing along a specific pathway; Bonhoeffer's theology grew as he asked and re-asked, '*who* is Christ for us today'?[3] Bethge roughly outlined three periods in Bonhoeffer's career, what he called Foundation (1927–1933), Concentration (1933–1940), and Liberation (1940–1945), and a primary aim of his lectures was to articulate how these seasons

---

1. Eberhard Bethge, 'The Challenge of Dietrich Bonhoeffer's life and Theology', in *World Come of Age,* edited by Ronald Gregor Smith (Philadelphia: Fortress Press, 1961), 22–88.
2. Bethge, 'The Challenge of Dietrich Bonhoeffer's life and Theology', 24.
3. Bethge, 'The Challenge of Dietrich Bonhoeffer's life and Theology', 43, emphasis original.

could be understood to cohere, even as he also recognized certain tensions between them.[4]

Continuity and Discontinuity

Continuity was an issue because—as Bethge noticed—Bonhoeffer's Finkenwalde writings (*Discipleship* and *Life Together*) raise particular interpretive dilemmas. He says, '[*Discipleship* and *Life Together*] are now held by some students of Bonhoeffer to mark a detour in his life, an unpleasant pietistic and legalistic narrowing of the pass'.[5] Liberals, as Bethge called them, had followed Hanfried Müller and claimed Bonhoeffer's religionless Christianity in favor of a Marxist worldview. Yet, this worldview did not reconcile with Bonhoeffer's view of the church. Both interpretive streams (those of Bonhoeffer's students and the other early interpreters) were confounded, and Bethge says, 'neither can make much use of this second period'.[6] Continuity issues consumed early Bonhoeffer interpreters, as John Godsey argued for a fundamental continuity between early and late (while recognizing important developments in the prison correspondence) and John Philips argued for a theological discontinuity regarding his ecclesiology and Christology.[7]   Hanfried Müller, himself author of an early controversial socialist interpretation of Bonhoeffer in *Von der Kirche zur Welt*, delivered a lecture in 1961 titled, 'Concerning the Reception and Interpretation of Dietrich Bonhoeffer', that drew attention to this crucial question.[8] The central point for all was figuring out this second period, what Bethge referred to as, 'Concentration'.

Clifford Green's monumental work *Bonhoeffer: A Theology of Sociality* was an important step forward in arguing for a fundamental continuity through the entirety of Bonhoeffer's corpus, as was Ernst Feil's 1971 work *Die Theologie Dietrich Bonhoeffers. Hermeneutik—Christologie—Weltverständnis*.[9] The issue persists into contemporary

---

4. Bethge, 'The Challenge of Dietrich Bonhoeffer's life and Theology', 24.
5. Bethge, 'Bonhoeffer's Life and Theology', 44.
6. Bethge, 'The Challenge of Dietrich Bonhoeffer's life and Theology'.
7. See John D Godsey, *The Theology of Dietrich Bonhoeffer* (London: SCM Press, 1960), 260–282; John A Phillips, *The Form of Christ in the World: A Study of Bonhoeffer's Christology* (London: Collins, 1967), 73ff.
8. Hanfried Müller, 'Concerning the Reception and Interpretation of Dietrich Bonhoeffer', in Ronald Gregor Smith, editor, *World Come of Age*, 182–214.
9. Feil's text would be translated into English in 1985 under the title, *The Theology*

scholarship too, as more recent treatments of Bonhoeffer's work, including texts by Sabine Dramm, Tom Greggs, Joel Lawrence, and Stephen Plant, continue emphasizing continuity over discontinuity.[10] And yet, in an interesting counterpoint which reveals continuity to continue being a relevant issue, Eric Metaxas's recent biography argues for an important discontinuity, and locates it within the prison correspondence.[11]

However, none of the authors arguing for continuity locate it within Bonhoeffer's systematic theology proper—specifically in an aspect of his doctrine of the Word of God—which directly ties *Discipleship* to Bonhoeffer's prior work. This essay shows how one can make

---

of Dietrich Bonhoeffer. Green and Feil, though giving different reasons, argue for a basic continuity within Bonhoeffer's thought. Green argues for continuity based on the concept of sociality. Though he notes an important moment of discontinuity with regard to *Discipleship,* the discontinuity is not theological but biographical, and Green points to Bonhoeffer's 1932 conversion to explain *Discipleship's* changes. Theologically, however, Green maintains that the sociality of faith retains its priority of place (Clifford Green, *Bonhoeffer: A Theology of Sociality,* revised edition [Grand Rapids: Eerdmans, 1999], 151ff). Feil, on the other hand, connects Bonhoeffer's early and late theology by understanding his continuous commitment to uniting theology and its concrete expression in faith (Ernst Feil, *The Theology of Dietrich Bonhoeffer,* trans. Martin Rumscheidt, [Philadelphia: Fortress Press, 1985], 53).

10. Sabine Dramm's argument for coherence is against the violence that categories such as, 'early' or 'late', 'man of piety' or 'man of the world' does to the rich complexity of Bonhoeffer's work. His thought must not be parsed out, for such differentiation would simply, 'do injustice to his identity as a theologian and a thinker, if not destroy it entirely' (Sabine Dramm, *Dietrich Bonhoeffer: An Introduction to His Thought* [Peabody, MA: Hendrickson, 2007], 2); Tom Greggs illumines Bonhoeffer's theological continuity through the concept of religionless Christianity, saying, '[t]here is . . . a significant level of continuity between these later thoughts [on religionless Christianity] and concerns that Bonhoeffer had from his earliest days as a theologian' (Tom Greggs, *Theology Against Religion: Constructive Dialogues with Bonhoeffer and Barth,* [London: T&T Clark, 2011], 42); Joel Lawrence's treatment of Bonhoeffer's theology, in which he uses his early writing to extrapolate his later writing, presupposes a continuity that allows the early material to inform the later. See Joel Lawrence, *Bonhoeffer: A Guide for the Perplexed;* Stephen Plant treats *Discipleship* as a seamless theological unity, noting that Bonhoeffer's exposition of Pauline theology is 'Feeding off his doctoral dissertation' (Stephen Plant, *Bonhoeffer* (London: T&T Clark, 2004), 104).

11. Eric Metaxas, *Bonhoeffer: Pastor, Martyr, Prophet, Spy: A Righteous Gentile vs. the Third Reich* (Nashville: Thomas Nelson, 2010), 465–468.

use of this second period by demonstrating substantial theological harmonies with Bonhoeffer's early, academic work. I contend that *Discipleship* is radically dependent upon Bonhoeffer's earlier work, especially sections from his 1932-1933 theological anthropology lectures, his 1932 lecture, 'Christ and Peace', *Act and Being*, and *Sanctorum Communio*. Even as *Discipleship's* rhetoric and form of argumentation is obviously quite different, the central *theological* points he asserts are very compatible with his prior theological work. Therefore much should be made of this season—precisely because of these continuities.

The essay begins with a reading of his theses on 'Faith and Devotion' and 'Obedience and Action' from his theological anthropology lectures, highlighting substantial theological points so as to highlight their presence in *Discipleship*. It then gives a reading of salient aspects of *Discipleship's* early chapters, drawing attention to the theological continuities with his early work. This, in turn, not only establishes continuity between the two but also provocatively addresses an issue within *Discipleship* interpretation proper. Interpreters of no less stature than Eberhard Bethge, Clifford Green, John Godsey, and Geffrey Kelly have noted *Discipleship's* roots in Bonhoeffer's November 1932 lecture, 'Christ and Peace', but fail to also note the overwhelming similarities between his November 1932 – February 1933 lectures in theological anthropology—which themselves share remarkable similarities with *Act and Being*.[12] Linking the texts together in this manner demonstrates that *Discipleship's* roots extends beyond one lecture from November 1932, but rather comes from a series of sources through 1932-1933, and—precisely because of the theological anthropology lectures' use of *Act and Being* and Bonhoeffer's emphasis on God's *actus directus* for the life of obedience—extend all the way back to the late 1920's. Thus, this essay not only demonstrates Bonhoeffer's theological continuity, but shows *Discipleship's* conceptual roots are present in his dissertation and habilitation.

---

12. See Eberhard Bethge, *Dietrich Bonhoeffer: A Biography*, revised edition, edited by Victoria J Barnett (Minneapolis: Fortress Press, 2000), 457; Clifford Green, *Bonhoeffer: A Theology of Sociality*, 150–151; Geffrey B Kelly and John D Godsey, 'Editor's Introduction to the English Edition', in Bonhoeffer, *Dietrich Bonhoeffer Works*, volume 4 *Discipleship*, edited by Geffrey B Kelly and John D Godsey, translated by Reinhard Krauss and Barbara Green (Minneapolis: Fortress Press, 2001), 5. Hereafter cited as *DBWE* 4.

The central elements of continuity between Bonhoeffer's theological anthropology lectures and *Discipleship* begin with his theses on 'Faith and Devotion'. These theses place awareness in faith—the consciousness of faith in reflection—and its relationship to the continuity of being in conversation as Bonhoeffer speaks of faith as *actus directus* and devotion as *actus reflexus*. The central point the theses assert is that faith is a function of *actus directus*, and devotion a function of *actus reflexus*. These points, by and large, are a reiteration of the tensions *Act and Being* raised and resolved, specifically the issue of continuity of human being in light of faith as *actus directus*.[13] Faith and devotion naturally raise issues of continuity of being because faith is described as a regenerative act, and one legitimately questions how being is a continuous whole in light of God's regeneration.[14] The theses sketch Bonhoeffer's middle ground of describing faith as God's free act, and creates the awareness of God's work in Christ such that Christians can live a new way of being and yet does not renew humanity at the level of being beyond Christ's work in the resurrection.[15] This is important for three reasons. In the first instance, it reveals that Bonhoeffer's theological priorities from *Act and Being* are still present in these Berlin lectures. Secondly, it is

---

13. Dietrich Bonhoeffer, *Dietrich Bonhoeffer Works*, volume 12, *Berlin: 1932-1933*, edited by Larry L. Rasmussen, translated by Isabel Best and David Higgins (Minneapolis: Fortress Press, 2009), 221. Hereafter cited as *DBWE* 12. By faith as *actus directus* or *actus reflexus*, Bonhoeffer is highlighting the question as to whether the 'act of faith rests on the objectivity of the event of revelation in Word and sacrament' (Bonhoeffer, *Dietrich Bonhoeffer Works*, volume 2 *Act and Being: Transcendental Philosophy and Ontology in Systematic Theology*, edited by Wayne Whitson Floyd, translated by H Martin Rumscheidt [Minneapolis: Fortress Press, 1996], 158. Hereafter cited as *DBWE* 2), or as the 'reflexive answer of consciousness' to God's work (*DBWE* 2:159). See *DBWE* 2:158–160 for Bonhoeffer raising the issue of *actus directus* vs. *actus reflectus*.
14. This is why thesis three restates the argument regarding continuity of personhood which *Act and Being* set forth. See *DBWE* 12:221 and *DBWE* 2:96–103.
15. This is a central argument of *Act and Being*, extensively developed in Part C (136 ff). For Bonhoeffer, the gift of faith is not a metaphysical transition in being, but a perceptive renewal as the individual can now, for the first time, live in authenticity to her potential-to-be in Christ instead of herself. See also the beginning of the *Ethics* manuscript 'Ultimate and Penultimate Things', as Bonhoeffer describes justification with reference to renewal of *vision* which results in freedom, and not a renewal at the level of being. See Bonhoeffer, *Dietrich Bonhoeffer Works*, volume 6 *Ethics*, edited Clifford J Green, translated Reinhard Krauss, Charles C West, and Douglas W Stott (Minneapolis: Fortress Press, 2005), 146.

important because his overt connection to *Act and Being* continues into the theses on "Obedience and Action", though not as obviously drawn. Finally, the material points the theses establish regarding faith as God's *actus directus* undergird key aspects of *Discipleship's* initial arguments.

Theses on Obedience and Action

Bonhoeffer's theses on 'Obedience and Action' make a clear conceptual link between *Act and Being's* theological structure and *Discipleship's* material content as they sketch how obedience remains *actus directus* and action *actus reflexus*. Just prior to Bonhoeffer's theses on 'Obedience and Action' there is a very short collection of notes entitled 'Obedience and doing works. Paper by Tillich', which he apparently presented by way of introduction. He seems to have juxtaposed the perspective advocated in the Tillich paper (it is unknown if it is a paper by student Ernst Tillich or a report on a paper by Paul Tillich) because it emphasizes the role of the individual in obedience. Bonhoeffer frames the issue saying, 'What is the relation between the obedient nature of the human being as *actus directus* and concrete acts [to] doing the act as *actus reflexus*?'[16] He then begins his eight theses demonstrating obedience as *actus directus* by discussing the relationship between obedience and belonging (theses 1 and 2), then the relationship between hearing, acting, and obedience (theses 3–6). The theses conclude with two remarks regarding the relationship between obedience and hearing the Word of God in faith (theses 7–8). Taken as a whole, the theses assert that obedience, faith, and action are an inseparable whole, and that all are a function of God's free action.

Bonhoeffer frames his argument in thesis one and two by tying obedience to belonging, 'in the form of hearing',[17] and he does so because of how he understands hearing God. One does not merely listen to God's word spoken over them and then act. Rather, belonging to God—obedience—is a theologically complex moment in which God's Word, as the *verbum visible*, 'creates in the hearing what it

---

16. *DBWE* 12:226.
17. *DBWE* 12:226.

represents'.[18] Thus, as God's word is proclaimed it creates faith as the action of the creative Word of God.

Theses three through six develop the relationship between hearing and acting, and link hearing the Word of God with responsible action. Bonhoeffer specifically addresses how one interprets obedience and action—and its significance—by critiquing dynamic instrumentalism, and by this he is rejecting an interpretation of human behavior and God's creative word.[19] Dynamic instrumentalism, or pragmatism, begins with interpreting an action, and then deducing that because one has acted, then one has heard, which therefore implies the activity of the Word of God. A phenomenology which runs the logic of experience backwards and deduces God's activity is precisely the misunderstanding Bonhoeffer fervently desires to avoid when treating obedient action in Christian life. His aversion to pragmatism has two root causes. First, an instrumentalist interpretation tempts the conclusion that acting is subsequent to hearing because one must hear the word of God before one acts. This plunges the individual back into the problem of act and being, the solution to which his theses on 'Faith and Devotion' recapped.

Secondly, Bonhoeffer criticizes instrumentalism because, 'it is an image inappropriate to the facts . . . because in it the fundamental opposition of God and the human being is dissolved and thus mysticism (mysticism of the will, of sanctification) is unavoidable'.[20]

---

18. *DBWE* 12:226.
19. *DBWE* 12:226. Instrumentalism, as a philosophical school, closely parallels pragmatism. For an example of the type of religious philosophy Bonhoeffer was rejecting, see William James, 'The Varieties of Religious Experience', especially lectures IX, X, and XX in *William James: Writings 1902–1910*, edited by Bruce Kuklick (New York: The Library of America, 1987), 177–238 and 435–463 respectively. See also Bonhoeffer's critique of pragmatism and instrumentalism in Bonhoeffer, *Dietrich Bonhoeffer Works*, volume 10, *Barcelona, Berlin, New York: 1928–1931*, edited by Clifford S Green, translated by Douglas W Stott (Minneapolis: Fortress Press, 2008), 310–312, hereafter cited as *DBWE* 10, and his specific critique of James and the 'Varieties of Religious Experience' in *DBWE* 10:438–440. In addition, see Ralf Wüstenberg's discussion on William James's long-term philosophical influence on Bonhoeffer in 'Philosophical Influences on Bonhoeffer's 'Religionless Christianity', in *Bonhoeffer and Continental Thought: Cruciform Philosophy*, edited by Jens Zimmerman and Brian Gregor (Bloomington: Indiana University Press, 2009), 137–155.
20. *Bonhoeffer and Continental Thought: Cruciform Philosophy*.

In effect, Bonhoeffer says that running the logic of experience backwards necessitates the inward turn of reflection as a source of knowledge. Hence, he says it dissolves in mysticism. Thus dynamic instrumentalism is rejected because it is both theologically insufficient and methodologically treacherous.

Bonhoeffer's concern is that, when one establishes a phenomenological structure of interpretation, not only does it theologically separate hearing and acting, but the individual becomes central instead of God. This inward turn of mysticism means that acting is always secondary to hearing, as one first must turn inward and discern God's speech. This goes against a central presupposition driving Bonhoeffer's theology: the human source of knowledge is God's *external action* upon the individual, not personal contemplation. The central divide represented by the *cor curvum in se* dissolves as human contemplation becomes the central point of reference for revelation, opening up a litany of concerns he addressed both earlier in the lectures and also in *Act and Being* and *Sanctorum Communio.* Thus, the thesis ends with a strong counter word against an instrumentalist interpretation as he says, 'Hearing *is* acting'.[21]

After protecting and mitigating against a self-centered phenomenology of interpretation, thesis four explores the anthropological implications of a unified address by the word of God. And here, Bonhoeffer is keen to uphold the unity of being he established by working with the philosophical category of *Dasein* in his theses on 'Faith and Devotion' and *Act and Being.* He says, 'If hearing is originally acting, then the word is something that addresses the human being in his entire existence, body and soul; then the human being is still undivided in pneuma, nouj, swma, in hearing and doing, passivity and activity, in act and being'[22] Bonhoeffer maintains the

---

21. *Bonhoeffer and Continental Thought: Cruciform Philosophy*, emphasis original.
22. *Bonhoeffer and Continental Thought: Cruciform Philosophy.* Though beyond the purview of this essay, there are many significant philosophical implications in Bonhoeffer's adoption of *Dasein* as a category for discussing theological anthropology. One of these is his commitment to the unity of humanity at the level of being. This is an area where one must pay careful attention to Bonhoeffer's intentional adoption of the philosophical category of *Dasein* and its implications. Thus, we quickly note an aspect of *Dasein* in the work of Martin Heidegger. Heidegger rejects spirit, consciousness, and soul as 'things' which could be discussed in the context of being. Heidegger says, 'All these terms refer to definite phenomenal domains which can be "given form" ['*ausformbare*']: but

complete unity of spirit, mind, and body, and in human being.

How can the word heard be understood to translate into action without devolving into instrumentalism? Bonhoeffer's answer lies in action based on reflection, and he develops his thought through a three tiered way one can reflect. He says, 'First: I know myself before God in devout acts; the second: theological reflection on the heard word and the act; the third: practical reflection on the consequences of that which has been heard.'[23] Very importantly, it is only the third level of reflection which leads to action. One can reflect on the standing they have before God through their behavior, and one can theologically reflect upon their encounter with God. However, neither move toward action because both rely on the self as the arbiter of meaning. Only reflection on the *consequences* of what has been heard moves one to action. This, in turn, allows Bonhoeffer to bring his argument full circle through his seventh and eighth theses.

Thesis seven reinforces that obedience is a function of God's direct action and not of human reflection. The thesis begins, 'Obedience remains *actus directus*,'[24] and he immediately ties obedience into the third level of reflection. He says:

> In hearing the word, the human being, as one who is aware of his original unity in faith, knows that he is simultaneously called to the impossibility of achieving this unity and to do something. This act ... is obedience, is *actus directus*, to the extent that its necessity and impossibility are known in the same manner, i.e., to the extent that it occurs in faith.[25]

---

they are never used without a notable failure to see the need for inquiring about the Being of the entities thus designated. *So we are not being terminologically arbitrary when we avoid these terms*—or such expressions as "life" and "man"—in designating those entities which we are ourselves.' (Martin Heidegger, *Being and Time*, translated by John Macquarrie and Edward Robinson [Oxford: Blackwell, 1962], 72), emphasis mine. For Heidegger, matters of soul are inconsequential and summarily ignored, precisely because they posit a substance of—instead of an interpretation of—existence. Bonhoeffer's emphasis on the unity of being and his use of *Dasein* as a category reveals his fundamental agreement with Heidegger here.

23. *Bonhoeffer and Continental Thought: Cruciform Philosophy.*
24. *Bonhoeffer and Continental Thought: Cruciform Philosophy.*
25. *Bonhoeffer and Continental Thought: Cruciform Philosophy.*

To the extent that action is done in faith—behavior based on reflection upon what has occurred through encountering the Word of God in Christ—it remains *actus directus*. Christians belong to God by right of hearing God's Word, and they perform acts of obedience as a consequence of belonging to God. Readers will note that all of this theologically positions Bonhoeffer for *Discipleship*, in which he develops a rich understanding of the life of simple obedience—belonging to Christ—signified by reflection on Christ's call to follow and its inherent imperatives for daily life. Thus, this essay is now poised for a close reading of *Discipleship* so as to reveal these very dynamics at work.

Discipleship

A familiarity with Bonhoeffer's technical theological work illumines that *Discipleship's* early chapters not only possess a surprising level of theological precision, but this precision comes directly from his early, academic theology. Even as there are undoubted rhetorical differences, *Discipleship's* undergirding theology remains the same.[26] This essay's second portion looks into the theology underneath *Discipleship* to reveal the theological harmonies between this text and Bonhoeffer's earlier work. It begins with its second chapter, the 'Call to Discipleship'.

Discipleship's second chapter links the significant points his theses on 'Obedience and Action' established with the anthropology he argued in *Act and Being* and his inaugural lecture at Berlin. As he says, 'Faith is possible only in this new state of existence created by obedience. This first step should, to begin with, be viewed as an external deed which exchanges one mode of existence for another'.[27] As he very clearly explicated in *Act and Being's* Part C, 'mode of existence' language implies a precise theological anthropology, even as he never develops the point in *Discipleship*; this linguistic turn of phrase is by no means accidental. Thus, Bonhoeffer establishes a clear, though by no means overt, connection with central theological

---

26. This argument for continuity is made with particular poignancy by Sabine Dramm, as she speaks of theological links between Bonhoeffer's early work and *Discipleship*, while recognising a very different form of argumentation. See Sabine Dramm, *Bonhoeffer: An Introduction to His Thought*, 80–81.

27. *DBWE* 4:64.

points which underscore much of his academic work. Discipleship—Christian life as the unity of faith and obedience as a result of God's inbreaking *actus directus*—allows the individual to live in a new mode of being, as a Christ follower. This first step of obedience should be understood as the external deed (that is, act) through which one constitutes one's existence (that is, being) in the mode of Christ from the mode of Adam.

With this in mind, we can understand why Bonhoeffer develops the call to discipleship as he does through his extrapolation of Mark 2:14. In the idiom of his previous work, *Discipleship* develops Christ's call in reference to God's *actus directus*, God's creative *verbum visibile*. Though he does not use academic language to state that God's direct action of encounter is a creative word that creates what it says, nonetheless, what he does say is, 'A call to discipleship thus immediately creates a new situation'.[28] This new situation, in the biblical narrative, was the calling of Levi the tax collector to leave his booth and the call for Peter to leave his nets; it was the new situation Christ established in which they learned to have faith through obedience. Alluding to the more substantial Christology undergirding his point, Bonhoeffer highlights the significance of the call coming from Jesus himself. He says, 'Because Jesus is the Christ, it has to be made clear from the beginning that his word is not a doctrine. Instead, it creates existence anew'[29] The Messiah's call creates the conditions for the unity of faith and obedience because Jesus' call is God's creative word.

Bonhoeffer develops the intricate relationship between faith and the initial step of obedience, saying, 'The first step puts the follower into the situation of being able to believe',[30] and he ties it into the mutually constitutive relationship between faith and obedience.

---

28. *DBWE* 4:62.
29. *DBWE* 4:62. This point draws attention to the fact that Bonhoeffer's emphasis is on Christ's creative word and not a narrative formulation which Christians must imitate. This becomes more apparent when one recalls that Christ's call to discipleship comes through baptism, particularly infant baptism. *DBWE* 4:88, 205–212. For Bonhoeffer's account of baptism and in relationship to creating existence anew, see his defense of infant baptism at Bonhoeffer, *Dietrich Bonhoeffer Works*, volume 16, *Conspiracy and Imprisonment: 1940-1945*, edited by Mark S Brocker, translated Lisa E Dahill, (Minneapolis: Fortress Press, 2006), 551–572.
30. *Dietrich Bonhoeffer Works*, volume 16, *Conspiracy and Imprisonment: 1940-1945*.

Thus, an awareness of Bonhoeffer's substantial work regarding God's creative word fills out the theology underneath this narrative exegesis. *Discipleship* speaks of the unity of faith and obedience by noting that those who obediently follow Christ have learned to have faith. They obey his call by following in that very moment of faith the call creates, and this is how Bonhoeffer arrives at his famous assertion that, '*Only the believers obey,* and *only the obedient believe*'.[31] Thus, though *Discipleship* only subtly hints at his prior theological work's presence, Bonhoeffer has theologically shown Jesus' call to discipleship as God's *actus directus* and the creative word that creates faith.

Discipleship goes on to offer an extended discussion on the relationship between faith and obedience—something his academic work extensively treats—though Bonhoeffer still only uses the biblical narrative to expound the relationship. This is, again, something well-conceived in his prior work. *Act and Being* was preoccupied with similar types of questions, and all his theses on 'Obedience and Action' are centrally concerned with the mutually constitutive relationship between faith and obedience and its relationship to God's creative word. *Discipleship* continues this discussion, only now through the vocabulary of '*Nachfolgen*'.

Bonhoeffer's treatment of the relationships between faith, obedience, and action are distinctly present in his exegesis of Luke 9:57–62. Here, *Discipleship* provides a criticism of the three different responses to Christ's call by effectively focusing upon improper reflection on encountering God. In his theses on 'Obedience and Action', Bonhoeffer noted that a 'practical reflection on the consequences of that which has been heard',[32] moves the word heard into action, and *Discipleship's* logic follows the same structure. The first would-be disciple, whom Bonhoeffer labels as an enthusiast, comes to Christ with his own agenda, something which he does not specifically address in the theses.[33] However the second disciple's

---

31. *Dietrich Bonhoeffer Works*, volume 16, *Conspiracy and Imprisonment: 1940–1945*, 63, emphasis original.
32. *DBWE* 12:227.
33. Spiritual enthusiasm, however, has been a persistent foil for Bonhoeffer over time. See *DBWE* 1:250, *DBWE* 2:154, *DBWE* 10:448, and *DBWE* 12:205 for various critiques of enthusiasm. See also Bonhoeffer's recurrent comments against enthusiasm in the Bethel Confession at *DBWE* 12:376–378, 386, 400, and 410.

Joseph McGarry 25

desire to fulfill the law before following Christ parallels Bonhoeffer's first level of reflection (which does not lead to action) that, 'I know myself before God in devout acts.'[34] The devout act of fulfilling the law, which gave the would-be disciple position before Christ, is not discipleship. In fact, Jesus opposes the disciple's status before the law by calling the man to follow here and now. The man's refusal in the biblical account corresponds with Bonhoeffer's prior view that this level of reflection does not lead to action, that is discipleship.

The third would-be disciple is denied by Christ because he sets his own conditions for following. This, again, coincides with Bonhoeffer's second level of reflection (which also does not lead to action), 'theological reflection on the heard word and the act.'[35] In the biblical narrative, we see the would-be disciple choosing the time and manner by which he decides to follow Christ. Bonhoeffer emphasises how the third would-be disciple places himself both in the position of interpreting the significance of the call, and deciding the time and manner in which he will follow. In his academic idiom, the would-be disciple interprets the call and mediates its relation to action. And, again, this level of reflection did not lead to action in the theses and neither does it lead to discipleship in the narrative. This type of improper reflection is what Bonhoeffer spoke of in his lecture 'Christ and Peace'. There he said, 'Faith . . . must be simple; otherwise it will bring about reflection rather than obedience; the left hand will know what the right hand is doing and this is not discipleship.'[36] Consequently, we see hints of a very precise theological structure, one Bonhoeffer himself had already given four years prior in two sets of lectures, undergirding his biblical exhortations regarding the immediacy of obedience and the unity of faith and obedience.

Consequently, an awareness of Bonhoeffer's theological anthropology lectures is quite helpful in understanding the substantial theological work behind this dialogue and why the chapter unfolds as it does. His concern regarding the uniting of faith and obedience, and his rejection of a phenomenological—or chronological as he put it in *Discipleship*—interpretation, mirrors his earlier theological argument against dynamic instrumentalism. Bonhoeffer concluded the third

34. *DBWE* 12:227.
35. *DBWE* 12:227.
36. *DBWE* 12:259.

thesis on 'Obedience and Action' by highlighting the absolute unity between hearing and acting precisely because of the implications of God's creative word, the necessary inward turn when their unity is dissolved, and the consequent cheapening of grace. *Discipleship* raises the issue by saying, 'The very practical question remains open: when does obedience start?'[37] Bonhoeffer does not develop this issue in *Discipleship* as extensively as he does in the theses, and therefore knowledge of them proves helpful in understanding his treatment. The greater problem thesis three acknowledged is that only the *individual* can answer when obedience starts. Posing the issue by unlinking faith and obedience inevitably moves the locus of interpretation away from God's *actus directus* and toward the pietistic, inward turn. Or, as he put it, mysticism. Such a question makes the inward turn unavoidable, neglects the force and significance of God's free action over creation, and unhinges obedience from its essential relationship with faith. Though again, Bonhoeffer does not offer that rationale in *Discipleship*. Instead, he merely states that 'talk about obedience as a consequence of faith is unseemly, due to the indissoluble unity between faith and obedience.'[38] Yet, a greater awareness of Bonhoeffer's previous work illumines why this is so and reveals its import for this text.

Discipleship and the Cross

Bonhoeffer's fourth chapter, 'Discipleship and the Cross', is, perhaps, his most obvious moment of theological continuity with his earlier work, as it draws upon both the theological anthropology lectures as well as *Sanctorum Communio*. The obedient life is the life of suffering, and Bonhoeffer develops discipleship's suffering along three lines: the death of the old self, the war against the flesh, and vicarious, representative, burden bearing. Initially, he portrays suffering as the death of the old self in encountering Christ. This is because, 'Those who enter into discipleship enter into Jesus' death.'[39] This realization leads to Bonhoeffer's oft quoted phrase of, 'Whenever Christ calls us, his call leads us to death.'[40] And, again, the relationship between death

---

37. *DBWE* 4:64.
38. *DBWE* 4:64.
39. *DBWE* 4:87.
40. *DBWE* 4:87.

in Adam and life in Christ is one of the most abiding themes within his writings.[41]

This initial summons into death of the old self in baptism transitions into a second form of suffering, the war against the flesh.[42] Disciples participate in the suffering of Christ on the cross through the daily struggle against sin. This, itself, is a development of Bonhoeffer's work on Christian character in the theological anthropology lectures. Though the lectures do not use the vocabulary of suffering *Discipleship* possesses (save the language of bearing each other's burdens) he speaks of the practices of asceticism and the notion that Christian character is gained through such practice. This naturally lends itself to discussion on Christian discipline and individual struggle against the flesh.[43] There, he spoke of character formation as, 'Secondary, penultimate, yet significant as practice',[44] and detailed the practices that form Christian character in terms asceticism and exercises.[45] *Discipleship* develops these notions within a new biblical vocabulary. He says that temptation and the fight against the flesh, 'Brings Jesus Christ's suffering anew to his disciples'.[46]

Bonhoeffer is, again, linking daily Christian life to the costly grace of justification. Growing in Christian character, such that the, 'community is called to act in accord with their calling and identity in Christ',[47] means daily struggle. Discipleship is no justification of sin— thus, the text's opening salvo against the cheapening of grace—and simple obedience means constant and perpetual war against sin and the self. The theological anthropology lectures formally established what that struggle was, and *Discipleship* restates it here through the vocabulary of Christian identity, discipleship, and suffering, whilst also expanding upon the actual practice involved.

---

41. Joel Lawrence very helpfully emphasizes the centrality of death and daily dying in Bonhoeffer's thought, specifically highlighting its presence and importance in his early work. See Joel Lawrence, *Death Together: Thanatology and Sanctification in the Theology of Dietrich Bonhoeffer* (Unpublished University of Cambridge thesis, 2007).
42. *DBWE* 4:88.
43. This is precisely how Bonhoeffer addresses both spiritual disciplines and the Christian's sanctification later in *Discipleship*. See *DBWE* 4:158 and 262ff.
44. *DBWE* 12:232.
45. *DBWE* 12:232.
46. *DBWE* 4:88.
47. *DBWE* 4:262.

Bonhoeffer develops common burden bearing within the body of Christ for his third level of suffering. Theologically, he is restating two central aspects from *Sanctorum Communio*: the community bears one another in suffering, and this is understood as the church's vicariously representative existence.[48] Suffering in discipleship is not only individual (that is, both death in baptism and fighting against the flesh) but also communal. Bonhoeffer says, 'Christians become bearers of sin and guilt for other people . . . A Christian becomes a burden-bearer—bear one another's burdens, and in this way you will fulfill the law of Christ (Gal. 6:2).'[49] This leads him to conclude the central role bearing and suffering play in Christian life, a theme he has been developing through his corpus, and he explicitly ties it to Christian identity. Just as Christians have their being *Miteinander* in *Sanctorum Communio*, specifically expressed as burden bearing, so too he says in *Discipleship*:

> God is a God who bears. The Son of God bore our flesh. He therefore bore the cross. He bore all our sins and attained reconciliation by his bearing. That is why disciples are called to bear what is put on them. *Bearing is what constitutes being a Christian.* Just as Christ maintains his communion with the Father by bearing according to the Father's will, so the disciples' bearing constitutes their community with Christ.[50]

Bearing constitutes being precisely because Christians have their being in and with one another, specifically expressed through the sociality of communal burden bearing.[51] These are not casual lexical associations, and the careful reader can note that these subtle turns

---

48. Bonhoeffer, *Dietrich Bonhoeffer Works*, vol. 1 *Sanctorum Communio: A Theological Study of the Sociology of the Church*, edited Clifford J Green, translated by Reinhard Krauss and Nancy Lukens (Minneapolis: Fortress Press, 1998), 180-181. Hereafter cited as *DBWE* 1.
49. *DBWE* 4:88.
50. *DBWE* 4:90-91, emphasis mine. Note, again, the central position Bonhoeffer gives the practice of burden bearing as a practice that builds Christian character in *DBWE* 12:232.
51. See Bonhoeffer's discussion of this in his section on Christian life *Miteinander* and *Füreinander* at *DBWE* 1:178-184.

of phrase have very significant theological points of reference in Bonhoeffer's prior work. This, again, reveals the substantial theology undergirding Bonhoeffer's 'plain' exegesis, and it intricately links the content of *Discipleship* to his extensive academic theology.

Discipleship and the Individual

Chapter five, 'Discipleship and the Individual', expands on the significance of Luke 14:26. Itself, it is a reiteration of *Sanctorum Communio's* argument regarding the relationship between encounter and personal being. Bonhoeffer emphasizes the fact that Christ's call to discipleship is a person-constituting call, one which establishes the person as an individual before God and in community through Christ's mediation. Even as *Discipleship* reorders the presentation and begins with the individual person-constituting nature of encounter before its social person-constituting nature, the chapter—restated in *Sanctorum Communio's* terminology—demonstrates personal being as structurally closed and open through Christ's mediation.[52]

Bonhoeffer maintains the person-constituting logic of *Sanctorum Communio*, emphasizing the deeply individual significance of Christ's call, though now does so in reference to mediation. He develops the nature of discipleship by drawing attention to its necessarily social nature through Christ. This is, namely, that Christ's call makes individuals precisely so they will become individuals in community. As he says, 'It is precisely this same mediator who makes us into individuals, who becomes the basis for entirely *new community*. He stands in the center between the other person and me. He separates, but he also unites.'[53] This, of course, echoes *Sanctorum*

---

52. This introduces a subtle but important nuance within the treatment of discipleship and the individual, and reflects a different theological emphasis. *Sanctorum Communio* emphasized personal being in reference to God's work in and through the *community*, as Bonhoeffer was concerned with the constitution of the person in the sociality of faith. The *sociality* of faith was Bonhoeffer's primary concern. *Discipleship's* treatment emphasizes personal being in and through *Christ's mediation*. Thus, this text is less concerned with the communal structure of personal being as it is with the fact that all personal being is structured in and through Christ's mediation. And yet, Bonhoeffer's point regarding discipleship and the individual remains that there is a personal and social structure to personal being.

53. *DBWE* 1:98, emphasis original. Bonhoeffer doesn't intricately develop this

Communio's emphasis on the sociality of being in Christ and the church's structural centrality for human being. *Discipleship* reiterates the person-constituting relationship between being as structurally open and closed, though Bonhoeffer now lays most of his prior sociological work to the side and develops his case solely in reference to the biblical text and the significance of Christ's mediation.[54]

Conclusion

Taken as a whole, the initial chapters of *Discipleship* provide an exhaustive account of Christian life, such that those who encounter Christ's call are constituted individually and socially to follow in the simple obedience of faith which suffers. These chapters detail the 'what' of discipleship such that the remainder of the text can be seen as an unpacking of 'how' one follows in simple obedience. The crucial thing to note is that, in a very real sense, there is nothing theologically new here, and therefore no need to wonder how this writing comports with his earlier work. These chapters are the consolidation and reiteration of significant portions of his previous work, albeit in a very different form, as he eschews overt systematic structuring and appeals almost exclusively to the biblical narratives and their language. And yet, an awareness of Bonhoeffer's early career illumines the exacting and precise nature of his work, and its importance for locating the theology of *Discipleship* within his larger corpus. It is particularly important to recognize the parallels between his earliest work and *Discipleship* precisely because of how it pushes the "roots" of *Discipleship* further back than is most commonly noted. Though, as Bethge, Green, Kelly, and Godsey noted, the vocabulary of cheap and costly grace first appears in "Christ and Peace", the theological structure beneath it was in place well before. Furthermore, noting the substantial points of harmony between *Sanctorum Commuino* and the chapter, "Discipleship and the Cross" additionally buttresses this point. Demonstrating that Bonhoeffer's thought has not significantly

---

point in *Discipleship* as he does in *Sanctorum Communio*, but he does continue developing the theological relationship between the individual and community at *DBWE* 4:218ff and 234ff.

54. Surely this emphasis on Christ's mediation reflects how Bonhoeffer's thought developed, most likely, as a consequence of his 1933 lectures in Christology. See *DBWE* 12:300ff.

adapted or changed through this season—recasting his theology in more explicitly Christological terminology and biblical reference—reiterates he has, at most, reframed his work for a different readership. *Discipleship* represents no break which forces scholars to reconsider the work apart from a radically different rhetorical style. Thus, though Bonhoeffer's corpus is increasingly being understood as a coherent whole, this essay shows a fundamental theological continuity which rests in his doctrine of the Word of God, and not in secondary concepts like sociality, concrete application, religionlessness, or even *Stellvertretung.*[55]

In sum, an astute awareness of the theology underneath *Discipleship* reveals an overwhelming continuity with Bonhoeffer's earlier work. One which, precisely because if its *theological* nature, persists beyond the Finkenwalde years into Bonhoeffer's *Ethics* and prison correspondence and provides all Bonhoeffer readers with a way by which we can see his middle period hanging together with the rest of his corpus.

---

55. Bonhoeffer's identity as a theologian of the Word of God has been made quite clear by Philip G Ziegler in his recent essay, 'Dietrich Bonhoeffer: A Theologian of the Word of God', in Keith L Johnson and Timothy Larsen, editors, *Bonhoeffer, Christ, and Culture* (Downers Grove: Intervarsity Press, 2013), 17–38.

Vol 2/ 1 2014

Binding Sovereignties:
Dietrich Bonhoeffer and the Virtues

Dallas Gingles

Introduction

Dietrich Bonhoeffer's provocative and complicated conception of responsibility and freedom has intrigued scholars since the 1960's, with the first wave of critical work on Bonhoeffer, and is currently enjoying resurgence as we approach the seventieth anniversary of his death. Variously conflated with radical politics on the one hand, and contemporary evangelical cultural concerns on the other, the historical Bonhoeffer's participation in the anti-Nazi resistance is called as witness for any number of overlapping, and starkly opposing, political and ethical ends.[1] At the risk of wading into waters that are already too muddy, I will address Bonhoeffer's ethics of responsibility as related to the compelling story of his life and death with an eye to the political import of both.

---

1. The revolutionary image of Bonhoeffer began in the 1960's, going so far as to be reconstruct him as an early 'Death of God' theologian; that revolutionary image continues in current literature that considers Bonhoeffer's work as a prototype of postcolonial theology. On the other hand, the immense popularity of the Eric Metaxas biography, has given us a Bonhoeffer who fits easily into contemporary culture wars of American right-wing Evangelicalism. The mirror image of the Metaxas Bonhoeffer is the reconstructed pacifist Bonhoeffer of Mark Nation Thiessen, *et al*, who see Bonhoeffer as an anti-Niebuhrian ethicist who then fits easily into American left-wing Evangelicalism.

    For an example of the former, see Harvey Cox, *The Secular City: Secularization and Urbanization in Theological Perspective* (New York: Macmillan, 1966). For the latter two see, Eric Metaxas, *Bonhoeffer: Pastor, Martyr, Prophet, Spy* (Nashville, Thomas Nelson, 2010). Mark Thiessen Nation, Anthony G Siegrist, and Daniel P Umbel, *Bonhoeffer the Assassin: Challenging the Myth, Recovering His Call to Peacemaking* (Grand Rapids: Baker Academic, 2013).

The argument that I want to make about Bonhoeffer's ethics of responsibility is a fairly straightforward one. Rather than read his ethics as a kind of creative antinomianism, I will argue that a *qualified* virtue ethics offers a more coherent and plausible interpretation of Bonhoeffer's "venture of responsibility."[2] My approach, then, borrows from the critical development of virtue ethics that post date Bonhoeffer's work to make sense of his ethics of responsibility, specifically his conception of the 'free act'. I will begin by situating Bonhoeffer within theoretical boundaries by borrowing from Jean Bethke Elshtain's, *Sovereignty: God, State, and Self*, subsequently arguing that in Bonhoeffer's ethics, free acts are not unbound, but are bound to their agent.[3]

The Pretensions of Freedom and the Promise of Bonds

The late Elshtain was a political philosopher with sharp theological sensitivities. *Sovereignty* was her most systematic and sustained attempt to bridge the theological and political disciplines. This she did by rigorously analyzing the history of the idea of sovereignty, arguing that in the western tradition, the concept migrated from God to the state to the self. Each of these sovereignties exists in dialectic of 'bound' and 'unbound', with certain developments contributing to the binding and unbinding of the different sovereignties.

The final turn in her narrative is from the self 'bound' to the self 'unbound'. Promethean-like pretensions of selfhood disparage all bounds—religious, constitutional, and even bodily—as cyphers of repression, and, ironically, tempt selves to the most banal and original of sins: pride. Rather than willing oneself up by one's bootstraps into a new realm of heavenly delights, the self's reduction to will renders

---

2. The phrase 'venture of responsibility' is drawn from Bonhoeffer's claim that 'Freedom exhibits itself in *my accountability [Selbstzurechnung]* for my living and acting, and in the *venture [Wagnis]* of concrete decision'. Dietrich Bonhoeffer, *Ethics*, first English-language edition Dietrich Bonhoeffer Works (*DBWE*) volume 6, edited by Clifford Green, translated by Ilse Tödt, Heinz Eduard Tödt, Ernst Feil, and Clifford Green (Minneapolis: Fortress Press, 2005), 257 (emphasis original), and 283. For the exact phrase 'venture of responsibility' I am indebted to Robin Lovin. See, Robin W Lovin, *An Introduction to Christian Ethics: Goals, Duties, and Virtues* (Nashville: Abingdon Press, 2011), 230.
3. Jean Bethke Elshtain, *Sovereignty: God, State, and Self; The Gifford Lectures* (New York: Basic Books, 2008).

it incapable of anything other than the endless repetition of its all consuming desire.[4] This is an especially helpful way of telling the story of selfhood when situating Dietrich Bonhoeffer because it becomes readily apparent that whatever he might have meant by 'freedom' of act, he certainly could not have meant something that is reducible to the 'triumph of the will'. It was exactly this position he was out to destroy.[5]

Exactly how Bonhoeffer develops his understanding of freedom is a theme that helps us tie his ethics together from his earliest work through his latest. Bonhoeffer develops very important points in his later works that include the famous 'religionless Christianity',[6] and a 'world come of age',[7] but they also include, less famously, an appropriation of 'the natural',[8] a more substantive account of the good,[9] and a reworking of the Lutheran orders of creation.[10] The former have been major themes in Bonhoeffer scholarship, but any interpretation of Bonhoeffer's ethics of responsibility must also incorporate the latter into its analysis. The former makes Bonhoeffer's thought appealing in an era infatuated with postmodernity, but the latter makes Bonhoeffer's ethics compelling—plausibly even normative—across epochs. While we might live in 'a world come of age', the goodness of the natural world that Bonhoeffer articulates

---

4. Elshtain writes: '... proclamations of the sovereign self, whether in "hard" or "soft" varieties ... trace their genealogy at least all the way back to Augustine's debates with the Pelagians. Leading Christian theologians could never accept a doctrine of self-sovereignty, at least not until modernity, when some determined they could shoehorn the self into the box of sovereignty. By "hard" self-sovereignty, I refer to a maximalist version of such sovereignty. The "hard" or "maximal" version tends to be about power, self-encoded, enacted whenever the self sees fit. The self is both legislator and enforcer. The self is a kind of law unto itself, taking the form of a faux categorical imperative, faux in the sense that one could not coherently will that there be no daylight between one's own will and universal willing.' Elshtain, 172. For the full development of this position see, 149–246.
5. See Leni Riefenstahl, *The Triumph of the Will*. Film, 1934.
6. Dietrich Bonhoeffer, *Letters and Papers from Prison*, first English-language edition Dietrich Bonhoeffer Works (*DBWE*) volume 8, edited by John W DeGruchy, translated by Isabel Best, Lisa E. Dahill, Reinhard Krauss, and Nancy Lukens (Minneapolis: Fortress Press, 2010), 362–7.
7. Dietrich Bonhoeffer Works (*DBWE*) volume 8, 424–31.
8. Bonhoeffer, *Ethics*, 171–218
9. Bonhoeffer, *Ethics*, 219-98.
10. Bonhoeffer, *Ethics*, 388-408.

with increasing rigor gives us resources we need to pursue the good no matter the age of the world we inhabit.

Bonhoeffer's appropriation of naturalness, goods, and orders (what he develops into 'mandates') pushes his theology and ethics beyond the early Barthianism with which he is most often associated. I am not suggesting that Bonhoeffer 'gave up' on Barth. Instead, it seems as if Bonhoeffer's own theological contribution was to make Barthian divine command ethics accountable to the world that God had already commanded to *be*. In other words, God's will, if it is commanded, should be at least as lucid in the natural world as the commands of a deranged dictator.[11]

To approach this from a slightly different angle, we might say that in Bonhoeffer's ethics, along with the divine command, the created world becomes more intelligible, exactly because it participates in God's first and ongoing command to be and to flourish. The 'mandates' are God's primal command to human beings as a collective whole, and while their shape changes over time, their reality always remains embedded in the Word of God: they are 'grounded in the revelation of Christ'.[12] By anchoring these mandates in Christ, Bonhoeffer relocates the natural order into the divine Word. Rather than undoing the natural, this reframes the orders of creation in an 'ultimate'/'penultimate' dialectic that gives the penultimate *more* weight than it previously had, rather than less.[13] At the same time,

---

11. Michael DeJonge makes a similar argument about Bonhoeffer's earlier work. According to DeJonge, the early Bonhoeffer finds it necessary to rework fundamental Barthian notions of transcendence and revelation, in relation to categories of action, being, and person, in order to give them a basic relation to history and the world. See, Michael P DeJonge, *Bonhoeffer's Theological Formation: Berlin, Barth, and Protestant Theology* (Oxford: Oxford University Press, 2012).

12. Bonhoeffer, *Ethics*, 388.

13. In the first conclusion (there are two) of the letter where he writes of 'religionless Christianity', Bonhoeffer writes, 'In a religionless situation, what do ritual [Kultus] and prayer mean? Is this where the "arcane discipline" [Arkandisziplin], or the difference (which you've heard about from me before) between the penultimate and the ultimate, have new significance?' (*Letters*, 364-5). Rather than suggesting that a 'religionless' world is one in which ethical normative language loses all meaning or authority, then, Bonhoeffer sees such a world as one in which it is even *more* important to make careful claims about matters ultimate and penultimate.

the penultimate is also judged in relation to the ultimate, so that all human claims to ultimacy are exposed as empty pretentions.[14]

This relocated 'natural' makes ethical reflection possible in a way that is rather elusive in regular divine command ethics. In divine command ethics, the normal posture of the self might be construed as 'waiting'. God's command comes from the outside, to the self, in the concrete situation of life, and the only correct response is immediate obedience. These themes are all recognizable in Bonhoeffer's early and middle works. They are also present in his later works, but they exist within a different theological framework. Instead of the self's posture being one of pure waiting, the self is an active agent in relation to the mandates that mediate God's ongoing command (we might, once again, take this command at a highly abstract level as simply the command to flourish). For Bonhoeffer this ethical reflection is not 'ethics'. 'Ethics' is what one does when these mandates have collapsed. While this is a bit of a terminological gap for those of us who exist within guilds of professional ethicists, it is clear enough in Bonhoeffer's thought.[15]

At this point we can return to Elshtain's categories of bound and unbound to conceptualize Bonhoeffer's ethical self as 'bound' to the mandates that are God's command to all humanity. In this way the command of God to humanity is what makes humans human. Justifiable acts are acts that make sense within the world that the mandates convey to us. Put a bit more concretely, the mandates put parameters around our lives within which our actions and behaviors make more or less ethical sense. To put it even more concretely, for Bonhoeffer an ethical German person from his early life would probably have been just a pretty good German person all things considered: for instance that person's church attendance, obedience to civil laws, coherence within the culture, and proper familial

---

14. There is a complex kind of irony in Bonhoeffer's rejection of 'radicalism' as a way that the 'the relationship between the penultimate and the ultimate in Christian life can be resolved'. The radicals are those who reject the penultimate on theological (specifically Christological) grounds: 'Christ is the destroyer and enemy of everything penultimate, and everything penultimate is the enemy of Christ.' But in so doing, they deny the love that God has for the world—a love that is the *sine qua non* of the 'ultimate'. *Ethics,* 153–60.

15. Bonhoeffer, *Ethics,* 'The "Ethical" and the "Christian" as a Topic', 363–87.

relationships within which that person found him or herself.[16] The same would apply for, say, an America today. If one worships God, does not break the laws of the United States of America, follows the cultural norms of hospitality, arts, etc., and calls one's mother on Mother's Day, that one is probably on the right path for the good life. All of this is ethical so far as it goes.

Contrary to some more Barthian readings of Bonhoeffer, I think that it goes rather far. In fact, it is only because these mandates collapse that ethics properly speaking is a necessary practice for Bonhoeffer.[17] If one mandate begins to claim ultimacy for itself, collapsing the others into itself, it is at this point that the ethical person can no longer trust the world to mediate God's command for decent human flourishing, and the self becomes unmoored from its bindings. At this point ethical action becomes 'free responsible action'. This is not an immediate transition,[18] and Bonhoeffer does not want his reader to be glib about the demands of responsibility. In fact this is an ethics of limit cases, but the weight of Bonhoeffer's ethics rests on the norms of human flourishing, not on free responsible action.

The Demands of Freedom and the Limits of Ethics

Nonetheless, just because free responsible action is a limit case does not invalidate it as a real case. When ethical action must finally give way to free responsible action it is because the normal modes of ethical justification have collapsed. A world without functioning mandates is what Bonhoeffer calls 'twilight'.[19] Action in this world takes place in the darkness and the light, in the shadows, and in the gray area. This imagery is as provocative as is it is imprecise, and some of its provocative force rests in how accurately it portrays the

---

16. Bonhoeffer, *Ethics*, 364.
17. This is the logical relationship of the two final chapters in *Ethics*: 'The "Ethical" and the "Christian" as a Topic' (363–87) to 'The Concrete Commandment and the Divine Mandates' (388–408).
18. At least it is not immediate by necessity. It seems possible that such a state of affairs might obtain, but if the rise of the Nazi regime is not such a case, it is hard to imagine when the transition might be immediate.
19. Bonhoeffer, *Ethics*, 222 and 284. See also, Dietrich Bonhoeffer, *Creation and Fall: A Theological Exposition of Genesis 1–3*. Dietrich Bonhoeffer Works (*DBWE*) volume 3, edited by John W DeGruchy, translated by Douglas Stephen Bax (Minneapolis: Fortress Press, 1997), 104.

lack of clarity that is available to Bonhoeffer even as he is writing. If we were to push this direction, we might say that moral language has ceased to do its most critical work at just the point where it is most needed. In a move that he anticipates at least as early as *Creation and Fall*, Bonhoeffer has reached the limits of ethics.

These limitations are part of the ontology of human beings, and not simply reducible to limit cases and fallen mandates. External realities of the latter sort are but the most obvious iterations of the internal limits of human moral epistemology and finitude. As Bonhoeffer articulates it in *Creation and Fall*, the reasonableness of God's command to not eat from the Tree of Knowledge of Good and Evil is incomprehensible to Adam and Eve because they could not understand God's explanation that they will be 'like God . . . knowing good and evil', without already 'knowing' good and evil. This odd innocence falls away when they do eat from the fruit of the tree, and in this sin they come to know good and evil. However, their punishment is to live separated from the Tree of Life, whereby they had participated in the immortality of God's own life. In the Fall, they become like God in their possession of moral language, and unlike God in their finitude.[20]

This finitude goes all the way down, so to speak. It does not simply mark the mortality of human life—Adam and Eve were not like God in Selfsame plenitude prior to the Fall. They still had to eat of the Tree of Life to live. In this way their finitude was already part of their created state, being overcome—for lack of a better term—by God's bountiful gift of Life. Likewise, the moral language they came to share with God was still unlike God's, not in degree but in kind, because God's knowledge of the Good is perfect, while theirs comes about in the privative act of disobedience. So, the limit of moral language is, like finitude, part of the human condition, basically.[21]

Importantly, though, this basic condition of moral frailty is mitigated by God's command. What humans cannot know perfectly on their own they may hear from God. From the beginning to the end of his theology, Bonhoeffer believes that God commands humans, and that humans are responsible for simple obedience. As I have already argued, though, Bonhoeffer becomes continuously

---

20. Bonhoeffer, *Creation and Fall*, 80–93.
21. Bonhoeffer, *Creation and Fall*, 80–93

more confident about the normal conditions for human flourishing that God has commanded to be in the world. The created world is a commanded world: God commands the world to be and it is.[22] At the same time that God commands the world to be, God commands the mandates to enable natural human flourishing; thus, the natural world is occasioned in the Word of God.[23]

The mandates necessarily balance one 'with', 'for', and 'over against' another, and in so doing they reign in the human temptation to be for the self.[24] In the same way that sin is the refusal to 'be for others',[25] the collapse of the mandates is the refusal to accept the limiting function of the other mandates on any particular mandate. Ironically and tragically, when humans attempt to totalize their freedom by refusing any limits on either selves or any particular mandate, they undo the external conditions that were God's gracious gift for their flourishing, and the occasion for their true freedom. Unbinding the mandates unleashes totalitarianism.

This is the twilight. But the twilight is not an apology for the darkness. Concomitantly, just because ethics is, in this sense, a discipline of the twilight does *not* invalidate ethics as a task. In fact it makes it all the more important. Because moral knowledge and moral language become more intelligible in Bonhoeffer's appropriation of naturalness, goods, and mandates, it follows that, when these collapse, the appropriate response is not to accept the fatalism of the twilight and surrender to the darkness. The task is to hold whatever ground remains in the twilight, in the good faith that at some point it will be morning again. The attempt to hold that ground, though, is not an action justified and bound by the normal institutions of human flourishing; those have collapsed. So the attempt to hold the ground in anticipation of the morning must be a free act.

A word of caution is in order here, though, because 'free' does not mean 'good'. Those of us who live after the Allied victory in World War II, and after the collapse of the Soviet Union are tempted to

---

22. Bonhoeffer, *Creation and Fall*, 40–1.
23. See, Bonhoeffer, *Ethics*, 388–90.
24. Bonhoeffer, *Ethics*, 393–4.
25. Bonhoeffer, *Creation and Fall*, 62, passim. 'Being-for-the-other' is one of the most important ideas in all of Bonhoeffer's theology. See, Clifford J Green, *Bonhoeffer: A Theology of Sociality* (Grand Rapids: Eerdmans Publishing Company), 1999.

believe that 'freedom' is the ultimate human good. For Bonhoeffer this simply is not the case.

The freedom constitutive of Bonhoeffer's 'free act' is a precarious freedom that exists only because the normal bonds that rein in human will have collapsed. Free acts, then, should not be undertaken lightly. They are also acts that do not have the comfort of ethical justification, and therefore should not be undertaken presumptuously. Instead, they are acts that are meant to hold the ground between the twilight and the daybreak. And because they are acts of the twilight they can only be judged in the clear light of day. Ultimately this means in the light of God's final judgment, but also in the light of the new European world Bonhoeffer expects after the war.[26] These acts can only be judged *ex post facto*, and from the outside. How then are they not acts of unbound self-sovereignty?

The Bonds of Virtues

Because the free act awaits its judgment and possible vindication, it is necessarily in service to the reinstatement of the norms of human flourishing. If everyone only 'does what is right in his or her own eyes' we have only transitioned from antinominianism to anarchy. Given that the normal bonds that bind agent to good have collapsed, we must find some way to bind not only the free act to its agent, but that agent to good. Bonhoeffer provides one explicit example of this binding, and, I think, one implicit. The former is an immediate bond of good upon an act, and I will only mention it. I will then conclude with an argument for the latter.

The first binding good external to the free agent is the direct command of God. The freedom of God is not intimidated by the will of Hitler, nor confused by the collapse of the mandates. So, at any point, God can command an agent to act in any way that God so pleases. This is helpful so far as it goes. But it is not clear quite how far that actually is. The necessary and sufficient epistemic conditions for such an ethics seems very difficult to secure—especially if one is looking for an ethics that is meant to reinstate widely shared norms

---

26. I am indebted to Robin Lovin for this way of thinking about the dual judgment the 'light of day' will afford. Robin W Lovin, email message to the author, November 19, 2013.

of human judgment and justification, not simply an ethics for the individual.

The other possibility, only implicit in Bonhoeffer, is that a free agent is bound by his or her virtues. One way to conceive of this is to imagine that a free agent has unbound freedom only to the extent that he or she is ahistorical. While the anarchy of the twilight is a kind of rejection of history, the person formed by the divinely commanded realities of human flourishing carries those realities with them into the twilight, and as such, is free but bound. Bonhoeffer's own Lutheran heritage rightly teaches him to be suspicious about the abilities procured by virtue: virtue cannot justify. In fact, the strong version of this suspicion holds that at any point where one begins to trust virtue, one is in danger of the basest of sins, and is almost certainly deceived.[27]

Bonhoeffer's developed theology also gives us reasons to trust that the divinely commanded institutions of human flourishing can actually promote, and maybe even cause, human flourishing. Again, for Bonhoeffer, the moral person simply lives well within the mandates.[28] It is entirely plausible that such a person carries with him or her that same morality even when the mandates have collapsed. In fact, this seems to be how Bonhoeffer thought of the people most deeply involved in the anti Nazi conspiracies.[29]

This is a nuanced virtue ethics that does not trust the self to know its own virtues, and certainly not to appeal to them to justify its actions in the twilight. But, at the same time, properly functioning

---

27. See Jennifer A Herdt, *Putting On Virtue: The Legacy of Splendid Vices* (Chicago: The University of Chicago Press), 173–96.

28. 'The ethical phenomenon is a boundary event [*Grenzereignis*], but in its content and as an experience. According to both its content and the experience, the "ought" only belongs where something *is not*, either because it *cannot* be or because it is not *willed*. The fact that I live within the community of a family, of a marriage, within an order [*Ordnung*] of work and of property, is primarily a freely accepted bond in which the "ethical phenomenon", the ought, is dormant and not apparent in its objective and subjective sides. Only where the community disintegrates or where the order is endangered does the ought raise its voice, only to recede and fall silent again, once the order has been restored.' Bonhoeffer, *Ethics*, 366–67

29. See Elisabeth Sifton and Fritz Stern, *No Ordinary Men: Dietrich Bonhoeffer and Hans von Dohnanyi: Resisters Against Hitler in Church and State* (New York: New York Review of Books Collections, 2013).

mandates can secure enough virtue in the agent that those virtues set the course for responsible action *even when the agent cannot see those virtues operating.* This is rather self-evident at the most simplistic level, because it is inconceivable that Bonhoeffer would have been an ardent Nazi supporter. While this point might not have seemed evident to Bonhoeffer himself, we should not underestimate the weight that it carries. The responsible action seems to have something to do with a decision about how far into the resistance movement he should go. But the decision to not be a Nazi is one that he did not have to 'make' It was secured by his training in virtue. From the present vantage point, that virtue seems to have guided him all the way through, to the point that his decisions seem almost inevitable. Though they were free decisions of the first order, their agent was certainly predisposed to making them.

While this minimal 'virtue ethics' is not explicit in Bonhoeffer's work, he comes close to espousing something very like it when he writes about the freedom and bondage of the conscience.[30] 'In its content', writes Bonhoeffer, 'the law of the natural conscience corresponds remarkably closely with the conscience set free in Jesus Christ. This correct observation is due to the fact that conscience has indeed to do with preserving life itself and therefore contains basic traits of the law of life . . .'[31] The conscience, then, participates in the basic unity of the Word of God that is the command to humans to be and to flourish: 'the law of life'. In this way the conscience is bound substantially.

Prior to that substantial bond, Bonhoeffer argues that conscience is bound quasi-formally.

> [C]onscience . . . limits taking on and bearing guilt [Schuldtragen], which a particular responsible action necessarily entails. *First, the conscience freed in Jesus Christ still essentially remains the call to unity with*

---

30. This kind of virtue ethics could *only* be implicit in Bonhoeffer, as the resurgence of virtue ethics in moral theory was still decades away when he was writing. Given the development of virtue theory in both its philosophical and theological iterations, that Bonhoeffer's moral theory includes an account of the formation of the conscience that is an integral part of the formation of the ethical agent, only makes his account of the moral life more convincing.

31. Bonhoeffer, *Ethics*, 282.

myself. Acceptance of responsibility must not destroy this unity. Surrendering the self in selfless service[32] must never be confused destroying and annihilating the self, which would then also no longer be able to take on responsibility. The measure of guilt incurred in connection with a particular responsible action has its concrete limit in one's unity with oneself, in one's ability to bear the weight [*Tragkraft*]. There are responsibilities that I am not able to bear without being broken by them, whether it be a declaration of war, the breach of a political treaty, a revolution, or merely the dismissal of a single father of a family who thus finds himself unemployed, or, lastly, just giving advice in a personal life decision. It is true that the ability to bear the weight of making responsible decisions can and should grow. It is also true that each time I fail to meet a responsibility, I have also already made a decision for which I am responsible. Nevertheless, in the concrete situation *the call of the conscience to unity with oneself in Jesus Christ remains inescapable.*[33]

The unity of the self is the ground for free responsible action. The term "virtue" is too popular and ubiquitous to work out in detail how this account of the way that the conscience is bound by the unity of the self might map onto any given account of virtue ethics *per se*.[34] What seems clear, though, is that for Bonhoeffer, the external realities of any given case—even a limit case—do not reduce the ethical life to the running of a calculus nor to absolutism.[35] Instead the agent is free to act "on conscience," but only in a way that does not violate the

---

32. That is, in free responsible action meant to restore the mandates, and thus general human flourishing to their proper place.

33. Bonhoeffer, *Ethics*, 281–2. Emphasis added.

34. Any given virtue theory would need to account for the place of the conscience, the role of virtue in shaping an agent, and the relationship between that shaping, the agent, and the conscience. Only after such a survey and analysis could one begin to suggest the most promising account of virtue for Bonhoeffer's ethics. Such a project is well beyond the scope of this paper.

35. On these two poles see, Michael Walzer, 'Political Action: The Problem of Dirty Hands', in *Philosophy and Public Affairs* 2/2 (1973): 160–80, especially 162.

unity of the agent *qua* human, nor the law of life. To use the imagery above, the conscience that can bear the weight of the twilight is the conscience that has already been properly formed in the daylight. Likewise, the agent who has learned the habits of human flourishing in the world of properly functioning mandates is the agent who must use those habits even when the mandates have collapsed. And it is those habits that give unity to the agent, and it is by way of the unity of that agent that his or her act is bound—first by the agent, and finally by the good that formed the agent in the world that God commanded to be and to flourish.

Conclusion

The current world seems fascinated with the possibilities of unbounded freedom. Oddly enough, Dietrich Bonhoeffer has often been deployed as a theologian who supports such freedom because he resisted tyranny to the end. Irony can be an unpleasant friend, though. The tyranny that Bonhoeffer resisted to the end was the tyranny of unbounded freedom. It is not surprising, then, that Elshtain finds in Bonhoeffer the tools she needs to unmask and rebind just such tyrannies, what she calls "mini sovereignties."[36] And for a world that finds itself ever overreaching, seeking transcendence in the basest of imminence,[37] Bonhoeffer offers a gracious rebinding of will, a loving rebuke to the totalitarianism of being-for-the-self, and a set of tools we might wish to pull out of the box, sharpen, polish, and begin using to combat the fragmentation of a world congratulating itself that it has "come of age."

---

36. Elshtain, 159, and *passim*.
37. For this insight I am indebted to my colleagues Spencer Bogle and Nathan McLellan.

Hermann Sasse and Dietrich Bonhoeffer: Churchmen on the Brink

---

Maurice Schild

Introduction

In *Bonhoeffer Down Under* John Moses highlighted the coming of Professor Hermann Sasse to Australia.[1] Earlier Robert Banks had called him 'Australia's most distinguished acquisition from the Continental theological scene'.[2] However, Sasse's name is perhaps not well known beyond Lutheran circles.

Similarity and Diisimilarity

Like Dietrich Bonhoeffer, Hermann Sasse trained in Berlin and worked there as a pastor before the outbreak of World War II. He was Bonhoeffer's senior by almost ten years. The two men collaborated in Confessing Church causes. Contrast as well as fascinating convergences mark their different ways. Though both were baptised in the church of the Old Prussian Union, each readily and consciously identified as Lutheran. While Sasse would eventually join the Lutheran Free Church in Germany, Bonhoeffer was to be affected in prison by the knowledge that his name was not on the regular prayer lists of the remnant Confessing Church—whose fight, like Sasse, he had fought.

Dissimilarity is a dimension also *within* both men. Sasse's was 'a life filled with contrasts'.[3] His clear Gospel preaching still sounds sweet comfort to those who remember him; yet we read of 'this difficult man'

---

1. *Bonhoeffer Down Under*, edited by Gordon Preece and Ian Packer ATF Press, (Adelaide: ATF Press, 2012), 217.
2. *Colloquium*, No 2 (1976): 24.
3. Ronald Feuerhahn, *Hermann Sasse as an Ecumentical Churchman*, Cambridge (dissertation), 1991, 12.

even in more recent literature.[4] And Bonhoeffer, a special prisoner soon recognised and respected as bringing light and humanity into the gloom of Tegel gaol (1943) is himself puzzled how this 'brave front' of his can relate to the man he knows from within—with his 'feelings of resentment and discontent', his fears and longings.[5]

This paper will recall some biographical parallels, indicate a telling convergence or two of thought, and show the two theologians working on one significant project together. The parting of their ways thereafter is another story: Bonhoeffer's path so brief, to the point, and to a tyrant's revenge; Sasse surviving the war, but ending his European career soon after, and starting again in Australia. And, whereas the younger man 'had to have it all said' too soon, the older had time to reassess and restate his confession to another generation, another nation.[6]

Early Careers and Convergences

Both men received their theological training in the university of Berlin in what was the most 'ecumenically progressive faculty' in Germany[7] and at the feet of such renowned scholars as Adolf von Harnack and Karl Holl, Adolf Deissmann, and Reinhold Seeberg. Harnack's immense achievements as a church historian were enhanced by his work also in other fields and by the aura of his sheer brilliance as a teacher. Holl, already a student of Harnack, and a painstaking reformation scholar, initiated the 'Luther Renaissance' of the twentieth century.

In 1923 Sasse, already a pastor at Oranienburg near Berlin, wrote his dissertation with Deissmann, who held the New Testament chair and was 'the leading German personality in the young ecumenical movement'.[8] Bonhoeffer's 1927 thesis, with Seeberg, *Sanctorum*

---

4. Klaus Scholder, *The Churches and the Third Reich*, volume 2, (London: SCM, 1988), 137; see also Karlmann Beyschlag, *Die Erlanger Theologie*, (Erlangen: Martin-Luther-Verlag), 1993, 180.
5. *Letters and Papers from Prison*, edited by Eberhard Bethge (London: SCM, 1971), 39 and 347–349.
6. See Maurice Schild, 'Hermann Sasse's way: Scholar, churchman, immigrant', in: *Germans: Travellers, Settlers and their Descendents in South Australia*, edited by Peter Monteath (Adelaide: Wakefield Press, Adelaide, 2011), 384–401.
7. Eberhard Bethge, *Bonhoeffer: Exile and Martyr* (London: Collins, 1975), 78.
8. Eberhard Bethge, *Dietrich Bonhoeffer. Theologian. Christian. Contemporary*,

Communio, is famous for his insight into the nature of the church: 'Christ existing as community'.

The First World War had interrupted Sasse's theological studies. Of his company of 150 he was one of six who survived at Passchendaele! Twin to his awareness of such good fortune in returning alive from the Western front was another reflection: that the liberal theology of the preceding decades had become a casualty of the Flanders battlefields. The God of the trenches, it turned out, was not the calculable deity of the Enlightenment nor of nineteenth-century individualism.

Renate Wind writes how for Bonhoeffer too the war 'brought an end to an apparently sound world'.[9] Walter, one of his older brothers (second in a family of eight children), died of shrapnel wounds in France.[10] That deeply touched the sensitive Dietrich, and left its mark on his middle-class Wilhelmine parents and family.

In 1927 Sasse attended the first wold conference of Faith and Order, at Lausanne, and edited the total proceedings in German.[11] In 1932 Bonhoeffer became a member of the World Alliance for Promoting International Friendship through the Churches. Similarity and difference! But in the Germany of those years to be active in any such forums was not popular, and quickly became less so. Of his own involvement in the ecumenical movement Professor Sasse could later write: 'I gave more time to it than any other theologian in this country' [Germany]; and of Bonhoeffer his friend Bethge wrote that he is regarded as 'perhaps the greatest ecumenical figure in German Protestantism'.[12]

The Bonhoeffers suffered under no illusions about the rise of the Nazis. On the day Hitler took power (30 January 1933) Dietrich's brother-in-law entered the house with: 'This means war!'[13] Two days later, '... and in spite of the prevalent intoxication', Bonhoeffer gave a

(London: Collins, 1970), 49.

9. Renate Wind, *A Spoke in the Wheel* (London: SCM, 1991), 12.
10. *Dietrich Bonhoeffer – A Life in Pictures*, edited by Eberhard and Renate Bethge and Christian Gremmels, (London: SCM, London, 1986), 42.
11. Erich Renner, 'Biography of Hermann Sasse', in *We Confess*, volume 1, (St Louis: Concordia, 1984), 103.
12. Feuerhahn, as above, 65; and Eberhard Bethge, *Bonhoeffer: Exile and Martyr*, (London: Collins, 1975), 79.
13. Eberhard Bethge, *Dietrich Bonhoeffer. Theologian. Christian. Contemporary*, (London: Collins, 1970), 191.

broadcast on the changing concept of the 'Führer' (leader) and warned listeners that, should the leader 'allow himself to succumb to the wish of those he leads ... then the image of the leader will gradually become the image of the "misleader". .. the leader who makes an idol of himself and his office, and who thus mocks God'. Before these last sentences could be broadcast, Bonhoeffer's microphone had been switched off. The matter was never cleared up. But 'that was symptomatic at least', writes Bethge in the German original of his great biography (1967).

Sasse had pulled the mask away even earlier. Forever famous is the stand he took in the 1932 *Kirchliches Jahrbuch (Church Year Book)*, of which he was the active contributing editor. Here he declared that article 24 of the Nazi party program (which offered 'freedom for all religious confessions in the state, providing they do not endanger its existence or offend the German race's sense of decency and morality') made any discussion with the Church, any Church, impossible.[14] After that, publishing the *Church Year Book* was forbidden throughout the Nazi era.

Both Sasse and Bonhoeffer went out of their way to develop church connections and foster friendships in other lands and churches. America is perhaps the outstanding instance. Like Sasse before him (1925/26), Bonhoeffer travelled to the United States to broaden his experience and studies (1930). In fact, he found Sasse's critical report, *Amerikanisches Kirchentum* the best preparatory reading available at the time[15]. And like Sasse, he responded to the American experience with a quality piece which attracted many readers: *Protestantism without Reformation.*[16]

Both men spent time in Berlin as pastors who ministered to ordinary people. Their relationship to the church was certainly different from what was common a generation earlier, when it was not unknown for converts who had made their individual way to baptism, to be virtually left after that to work out their pathway into

---

14. *The Third Reich and the Christian Churches*, edited by Peter Matheson, (Grand Rapids: Eerdmans, 1981), 1–2.
15. See the English translation in *The Lonely Way. Selected Essays and Letters by Hermann Sasse*, volume 1 (1927–1939), edited by Ronald Feuerhahn, (St Louis: Concordia, 2001), 23–60.
16. *Dietrich Bonhoeffer Works in English* (Minneapolis: Fortress Press, Minneapolis) (hereafter *DBWE*) volume 15, 438–462. Also in *Dietrich Bonhoeffer*, edited by John de Gruchy (London: Collins, 1988), 195–216.

the church community also; '... many ministers had so little love for the Church themselves'.[17] Though working as a lecturer at the Berlin faculty, Bonhoeffer was also active as student chaplain, and rented quarters in the working-class area of Wedding to be available to his confirmees and to meet them on their own ground. And Sasse held the position of welfare pastor of Berlin in addition to his parish duties between 1928 and his transfer to the university of Erlangen theology faculty in 1933. At Erlangen this preceding 'school for life' continued in part-time service as hospital chaplain during the war. In Australia he was 'always the pastor'.

Church Unity and Plurality under Stress

Both Sasse and Bonhoeffer demonstrated growing respect for the Word of God, its unique inscription in the Bible, and its power to reform the Church. Hans-Siegfried Huss highlighted Sasse's memorable thetic statement: 'If we were agreed on what church and God's Word are, and in what relation they stand to each other, then nothing further would stand in the way of the churches uniting'.[18] This is not far from the promise of the Augsburg Confession, article 7. Bonhoeffer's similar insight, expressed to support preaching only on *biblical* texts also reveals this ecumenical horizon:

> 'The biblical text embraces the whole Christian congregation as a unity. It reassures us of our fraternal bonds not only with the congregation of Christ of all time past, and of the future . . . but with the total congregation of the present'.[19]

There are of course divergences of thought as well as instances of remarkable convergence between the two. Their differing accounts of their teacher von Harnack would be worth closer study. But in the 1930s 'the church's confession' rose to first rank of importance in theological discussion. Was a new common confession called for in the face of a common challenge, or were the official Reformation

---

17. Hans Ehrenberg, *Autobiography of a German Pastor*, (London: SCM, 1943), 113.
18. Hans-Siegfried Huss, 'Was heisst lutherisch?, *Jahrbuch des Martin-Luther-Bundes,42*, 1-22.[??]
19. *DBWE 10*, 350.

confessions of the Protestant churches to provide the bedrock for survival and the basis for their stand against the new heathenism of Hitler, a modern form of Manichaeism?[20] Sasse fully supported federated confessional churches giving their clear Christian witness; he was not for them signing away their identity, not for the sake of a superficial ecumenism, and certainly not because Hitler wished to have only one Protestant body with which to deal. And he was sufficiently committed to this stance to leave the famous 1934 Barmen Synod of 'the Confessing Church' in protest, alone. In 1985 Klaus Scholder wrote: 'For Sasse, who from the beginning was an uncompromising opponent of the Third Reich, the theological problems were more important than the political problems, while history is inclined to take the opposite view.'[21] (Bonhoeffer, who was serving German congregations in London at the time, had not attended Barmen).

Sasse, however, remained in the ongoing debate, maintaining his principle that '. . . a church in which another confession is recognised as having validity alongside the Lutheran confession has ceased to be a Lutheran church.'[22] The official confessions of the sixteenth century are neutralised to the degree in which the Barmen declaration is viewed as a common confession of Union, Lutheran and Reformed churches, and as leading to Communion fellowship (as then resolved in the Halle convention of 1936). On the Reformed side this may not have deep repercussions (on this Sasse cites Karl Barth); for Lutherans, he maintained, it sounds the death-knell of their church (see 'Wohin geht die altpreussische Kirche?')[23]

Bonhoeffer's letters show that he both understood and appreciated Sasse's position but could not finally agree. Bonhoeffer's view is concentrated on the event of God's Word occurring at the core of the Church. The divisions which had opened up across the Protestant churches confronted with Nazism resulted from the impact of the Word and followed lines other than those previously fixed. For that reason, he states in an important lecture in 1936, 'we can no longer go back behind Barmen and Dahlem [Confessing Church synods held in

---

20. Klaus Scholder, A *Requiem for Hitler*, (London: SCM, 1989), 97 and 169.
21. Klaus Scholder, *The Churches and the Third Reich*, volume 2 (London: SCM, 1988), 144.
22. Hermann Sasse, *Was heisst Lutherisch?* (München: Kaiser, 1935), 6, 7.
23. In *Lutherische Kirche*, edited by Gottfried Werner, Erlangen, 1936/1937, 92–94.

May and September 1934 respectively] . . . we can no longer go back behind the Word of God'. He maintains this stance even in view of his explicit further concession that 'the recognition of a "Confessing church with equal rights" is already a decisive breach of the Augsburg Confession'.[24] He states: 'The Confessing synod cannot stand up to the letter of the Lutheran confessional writings'.[25] In a letter to Barth a few months later he again acknowledges the importance of questions of substance between Lutherans and Reformed, and that the differences deserve much deeper exploration by a real expert, but regrets that 'Sasse's arguments are always utterly formal . . . '[26] Later, in a letter to Bethge, he returns to 'the Catholic question':

> 'How did we Lutherans get together with the Reformed? Actually quite *untheologically* (the theological formulation of Halle is really more a noting of the facts than a theological solution, which it certainly is not!); namely along two tracks: by God's leading (Union, Confessing Church), and through recognising what is objectively given in the sacrament: Christ as more important than our thoughts about him and his presence. Both questionable foundations theologically; and yet the church in faith decided for communion, i.e. church fellowship. She decided for recognising the Union as God's guiding; she decided to put her thoughts, her teaching about Christ back behind the objectivity of the presence of Christ (also in the Reformed Supper). But she did not unite *theologically* (except for Halle).'[27]

---

24. Dietrich Bonhoeffer, *The Way to Freedom*, Collins, London , 1972, 87–89.
25. *DBWE 14, 670.*
26. *DBWE 14* 255. Later, in Australia, he would remind his American friends both that 'The Confession is not object of legislation', and that 'doctrinal declarations are objects of the ecclesiastical legislation', thus, in the later instance leaving room for his understanding of the Barmen statement as well as the 'Theses of Agreement' underlying the 1966 union of the two Lutheran Churches in Australia (letter to JAO Preuss, 24 June 1964. Lutheran Archives, Bowden, South Australia).
27. BS 2, 380 [=*DBWE* 16,85; cf ibid 34 note 5] (emphasis added).

Sasse, 'an upright contender for the Lutheran confessional heritage',[28] brought the confessional question with him to Australia, where Lutheranism knew it well form its exodus and founding experience in the previous century. Here he was given a ready hearing. But the voice of Bonhoeffer on this matter may yet need to be heard.

Bonhoeffer's great love of the Lutheran Confessions is perhaps not well known. But Eberhard Bethge, who was present in his courses in the 'illegal' seminary at Finkenwalde in 1935/36, testifies that the *Smalcald Articles* were a favourite subject of his, and adds: 'In his final lectures of this series Bonhoeffer dealt exclusively with the *Formula Concordiae* . . . Every page of the *Formula Concordiae* in Bonhoeffer's copy... is covered with exclamation marks, scoring and question marks . . . He loved the *Formula Concordiae*'.[29]

Collaboration on the Bethel Confession

Before Barmen and its aftermath Sasse and Bonhoeffer knew each other from Berlin and from working together on *The Bethel Confession* at Bielefeld in August 1933. They acted as the chief formulators of a confession called for by Berlin theology students and pastors (who suggested both names) and by the emerging leadership of the coming 'Confessing Church'. It was a document intended to call Lutherans and others to order and to provide focus and mutual support in the face of Nazi bluff and brutality.

Looking back, Sasse wrote of 'a happy collaboration'. The English translation of Bethge's major biography, an abridged version of the German original, fails to convey Bonhoeffer's quite similar remark: he had 'joined in the work with real passion'.[30]

After Bethel, Bonhoeffer went to England, where he took up duties as pastor of German congregations in London (1933–34). Sasse had encouraged this move: 'I saw in him one of Germany's best

---

28. *Das Betheler Bekenntnis*, edited by Jelle van der Kooi, von Bodelschwinghsche Anstalt, Bielefeld, 1983, 11.

29. Eberhard Bethge, *Dietrich Bonhoeffer. Theologian. Christian. Contemporary*, (London: Collins, 1970), 368.

30. Eberhard Bethge, *Dietrich Bonhoeffer. Theologe. Christ. Zeitgenosse* (München: Kaiser, 1967), 354. The revised English translation, edited by Victoria Barnett and published by Fortress Press in 2000, follows the original and adds that Bonhoeffer said that he had 'truly worked with passion' (302).

theologians and did not want to see him go under in the petty war against the Gestapo and Rosenberg'.[31]

The genesis and – after the original drafters had left—the rewriting and demise of the Bethel Confession have been thoroughly described by Guy Carter.[32] Select invited responses delayed matters and led to a 'watered-down' version which Bonhoeffer, Sasse, and other co-workers would not sign. It was finally published at year's end by an understandably exasperated Niemöller, without other names. In its final version it consists of statements on:

1. The Reformation,
2. Holy Scripture,
3. The Triune God,
4. Creation and Sin,
5. Christ,
6. The Holy Spirit and His Gifts,
7. The Church,
8. History and the end of all things. A variety of topics at issue in 1933 are treated under sections 6 (among them 'life in the orders') and 7 (the holy office [the ministry], the state, the 'Volk', and 'The Church and the Jews').

It would be salutary to compare the two versions, the first reprinted after the war in *Gesammelte Schriften* (edited by Bethge) volume 2, 1959, 90–119, the final text edited and introduced by Jelle von der Kooi, *Das Betheler Bekenntnis*.[33] To mention but one example: in the first draft the Jewish issue is taken in its entirety, that is, without immediately limiting it to baptised Jews. Here the closing statement deserved to stand for all time: 'Christians who come from

---

31. Eberhard Bethge, *Dietrich Bonhoeffer. Theologian. Christian. Contemporary* (London: Collins, 1970), 230.
32. Ronald Feuerhahn, *Hermann Sasse as an Ecumenical Churchman* (dissertation) Cambridge, 1991, 78. See also Ferdinand Schlingensiepen, *Dietrich Bonhoeffer 1906-1945. Martyr, Thinker, Man of Resistance*, (London: T&T Clark, 2010), 134–135. On Sasse's role at Barmen see Enno Konukiewitz's study of another Lutheran leader in the Confessing Church struggle:*Hans Asmussen. Ein lutherischer Theologe im Kirchenkampf*, Gütersloh, Gerd Mohn, 1984, especially 92–95.
33. The two versions are now available in *DBWE* 12, 374–424.

the heathen world must rather put themselves in persecution's way than freely or under duress give up in any particular whatsoever the churchly brotherhood established through Word and sacrament'. But this sentence did not survive in the revision. The infamous 'Aryan paragraph', of which Bonhoeffer had early warning, had reared its head. On 5 September the 'brown synod' of the Prussian Union Church in Berlin accepted that non-Aryans could in future not become pastors! Bonhoeffer, now ready for separation, wrote to Barth, who thought the right moment was impending but still in the future and 'that the clash will come over an even more central point'.[34] Sasse's advice was to involve Lutheran bishops, especially Meiser of Bavaria. But how close Sasse's sympathies were to those of Bonhoeffer appears in his reply. He maintains that the Aryan paragraph

> . . . means that even the apostles of Jesus Christi, and moreover the Lord himself, who in the flesh was a son of David would have to leave the ordained ministry of the Prussian church. The new law indeed separates the Prussian church from Christianity. It amounts to blasphemy against the Holy Spirit, which cannot be forgiven either in this world or the next.[35]

The 'status confessionis', Barth agreed, had been arrived at (ibid 128-129). To Niemöller Bonhoeffer (together with his part Jewish ministerial colleague and friend, Franz Hildebrandt) indicated the need to have the synod dissolved and urgent doctrinal discipline proceedings to go forward, these to be headed by Sasse for the Lutherans, Barth for the Reformed.[36]

---

34. *DBWE* 12, 167.
35. *DBWE* 12, 169.
36. *DBWE 13*, 52–53. The relevant passage deserves to be citedas it stands:- 'What is indisputable now is for the synod to be dissolved immediately and for the entire church to be cleansed of this entire plague—solely according to the perspective of strict doctrinal disciplinary proceedings (with a panel of Sasse as Lutheran, Barth as Reformed)—and the strictest bar on membership, to clear out all the old and new half-baked Christians from our ranks. Precisely because this is about doctrine and not about jobs, it really doesn't matter if a few ignorant folk gossip about a chase for jobs. Who will believe that! Only Luther's language, not Melanchthon's, can help today . . .'

Such were the birth-pains of the Confessing Church. But the fate of the Bethel confession was symptomatic. When, all over the country, Jewish shops and synagogues were destroyed in the shameful 'Crystal Night', no church protested. In his work-Bible Bonhoeffer underlined Psalm 74: 7 ('They set your sanctuary on fire; they desecrated the dwelling place of your name') and noted 9.11.38 in the margin. Things had gone too far too fast. In the interim the euthanasia program had well-oiled the slippery slope to the full-out 'final solution': genocide for the Jews and other minorities. Not even the ecumenical world could help. In Australia Jewish refugees were interned, but—mercifully—not sent straight back to where they came from!

Bonhoeffer melded into the resistance (with other members of his family), 'escaped' to New York in 1939, then immediately and decisively turned back to his country: its fate, his fate. Sasse too contemplated exile and its ambiguities. In 1938 he was told he could go: 'but your wife and both sons remain here!' (Huss: 60).[37] He continued, and drew crowds of students to his classes, the highest theological enrolments at Erlangen occurring there in the 1930s.[38] In 1949 he, his wife and their two sons migrated to Australia.

Conclusion

Only if history is open for the future are these fathers in the faith 'now history'. Their progress beyond our place, one might say, lies not in being relegated but gathered up. Here their visibility is that of bold and gifted struggling sinners, there of the saints in light. Bonhoeffer's last words point to it directly: 'for me this is the end but also the beginning'. And in one of 'those sermons' [39], at Easter 1938, Sasse reminded his Erlangen listeners of the Lutheran Church's then 100-year sojourn in Australia, where Easter is *not* a spring festival,

---

37. Huss, as at note xviii above, 60
38. Karlmann Beyschlag,*Die Erlanger Theologie* (Erlangen: Martin-Luther-Verlag, 1993), 146.
39. Hermann Sasse, *Zeugnisse. Erlanger Predigten und Vorträge vor Gemeinden 1933-1944*, edited by FW Hopf (Erlangen: Martin-Luther-Verlag, 1979), 67–73.

Editor's Note: An earlier version of this paper appeared in *Lutheran Theological Journal* (1995, volume 29, 3–10).

but a celebration of *the light* of the new aeon. Every Sunday, each Easter, begins the new creation, all around the globe. Those who have entered that new beginning are right in the light – of which we glimpse the dawning. Already it is on our faces too.

Vol 2/ 1 2014

'Lord of the (Warming) World': Bonhoeffer's Eco-theological Ethic and the Gandhi Factor

Dianne Rayson and Terence Lovat

Introduction

Bonhoeffer's eco-ethic, emanating largely from his understanding of God who would be 'Lord of the World' in Christ, provides a framework for approaching the challenge of climate change. Whilst what can be gleaned of Bonhoeffer's eco-theology remains firmly grounded in his Christology, this paper explores the relationship between Gandhi's, and hence, Indian natural theologies, on the one hand, and, on the other hand, Bonhoeffer's own evolving natural theology concerning humanity's relationship with the rest of creation. The case rests partly on clear coincident thinking between the two men but also sufficient evidence in Bonhoeffer's writings to raise the question of this coincident thinking being more a case of Gandhi's direct influence on him. It is argued that Bonhoeffer's eco-theology, to be seen principally within the framework of his over-arching Christology but with unusually plain influence from Indian natural theologies, can serve to provide a suitable foundation for a contemporary eco-theology and allied eco-ethic that can assist the global community's search for solutions around the pressing issues associated with climate change.

The Ethical Issue: Climate Change

Climate change has been described as the 'great moral challenge of our generation'.[1] According to the best evidence available, the

---

1. Kevin Rudd, 'Climate Change the Great Moral Challenge of Our Generation', (Canberra: LaborTV, 2007); 'Faith in Politics', in *Bonhoeffer Down Under*, edited by Gordon Preece and Ian Packer (Hindmarsh, SA: ATF Theology, 2012).

changing climate is affecting human health and wellbeing, and indeed the security and sustainability of the entirety of the earth's ecology, with the most affected populations being among the poor, those least culpable and yet least able to effect mitigation and adaptation.[2] Furthermore, the effects are not limited to the poor: the health, productivity and safety implications of climate change are global.[3] The human suffering which this warming world is predicted to cause is of a scale unprecedented.[4]

Because the change in climate conditions is understood to be largely anthropogenic,[5] there is a clear challenge for it to be addressed by the human sciences as well as the natural sciences. If even partly an anthropogenic issue, then it concerns the way people live, their beliefs and behaviours. Among the human sciences that must address the issue is theology.[6] Even without the clear influence of religion

---

2. Alistair Woodward, Simon Hales, Navitalai Litidamu *et al*, 'Protecting Human Health in a Changing World: The Role of Social and Economic Development,' in *Bulletin of the World Health Organization* 78, no. 9 (2000); Camilo Mora, Abby G Frazier, Ryan J. Longman *et al*, 'The Projected Timing of Climate Departure from Recent Variability', in *Nature* 502, no. 10 October 2013 (2013); Intergovernmental Panel on Climate Change Working Group, 'Human Influence on Climate Clear, IPCC Report Says', in *IPCC Press Release 27 September* (2013).

3. Will Steffen, Lesley Hughes, and Sarah Perkins, *Heatwaves: Hotter, Longer, More Often* (Climate Council of Australia Limited, 2014); *Climate Change 2014: Mitigation of Climate Change*, edited by Working Group III, Ottmar Edenhofer, Ramón Pichs-Madruga *et al*, Intergovernmental Panel on Climate Change AR5 (Geneva: IPCC, 2014).

4. Martin Parry, Osvaldo Canziani, Jean Palutikof *et al*, *Climate Change 2007: Impacts, Adaptation and Vulnerability. Contribution of Working Group II to the Fourth Assessment Report of the Intergovernmental Panel on Climate Change* (Cambridge: Cambridge University Press, 2007); Koko Warner, Charles Ehrhart, Alex de Sherbinin *et al*, 'In Search of Shelter: Mapping the Effects of Climate Change on Human Migration and Displacement', (http://www.care. org/getinvolved/advocacy/migration_report.asp: CARE International, 2009), accessed 9 September 2013.

5. *Climate Change 2007: Synthesis Report. Contribution of Working Groups I, II and III to the Fourth Assessment Report of the Intergovernmental Panel on Climate Change*, edited by Core Writing Team, RK Pachauri, and A Reisinger, (Geneva: IPCC, 2007); Thomas F Stocker, Dahe Qin, Gian-Kasper Plattner et al., *Climate Change 2013: The Physical Science Basis. Working Group I Contribution to the Fifth Assessment Report of the Intergovernmental Panel on Climate Change* (Cambridge: Cambridge University Press, 2013).

6. Denis Edwards, *Jesus the Wisdom of God: An Ecological Theology*, Ecology and Justice: An Orbis Series on Global Ecology (Maryknoll, NY: Orbis Books, 1995);

on many of the beliefs and behaviours that, evidence suggests, have contributed to the anthropogenic dimension of the problem,[7] merely as a human science, theology must take its place as part of the public discourse about matters of global concern.[8] When one factors in the impact of the world's major religions, however, the onus on theology to reflect on its past and review its beliefs and their sources, becomes no less than a moral imperative. This applies especially to Christianity which, through its alliance with Western imperialist expansionism, imposed itself on so many parts of the world where apparently ecologically sustainable practices were replaced with ones now deemed to be part of the problem.[9]

We need, in other words, to address the issue theologically and develop a response which addresses both the causal factors and the consequences, including the theological dimensions in both cases. In Christian terms, indeed Abrahamic theological terms, the effects of anthropogenic climate change on the earth's flora and fauna, and on the entire inanimate portions of creation,[10] require an examination of concepts of stewardship and dominion, the relationship between human and non-human creation, and our very conception of who God is in relation to the world. In this context, it is contended that Bonhoeffer's notion of God, in Christ, as 'Lord of the World'[11] offers a valuable point of reflection, as does the possible influence of Gandhi on

---

Thomas Berry, 'Economics: Its Effects on the Life Systems of the World', in *Thomas Berry and the New Cosmology*, edited by Anne Lonergan and Caroline Richards (Mystic, Connecticut: Twenty-third, 1987); Celia Deane-Drummond, *A Handbook in Theology and Ecology* (London: SCM, 1996).

7. Thomas F Stocker, Osvaldo Canziani, Jean Palutikof, *et al*, *Climate Change 2013: The Physical Science Basis. Working Group I Contribution to the Fifth Assessment Report of the Intergovernmental Panel on Climate Change.*

8. David Ford, *The Future of Christian Theology* (Chichester: Wiley-Blackwell, 2011).

9. Core Writing Team, RK Pachauri, and A Reisinger, *Climate Change 2007: Synthesis Report. Contribution of Working Groups I, II and III to the Fourth Assessment Report of the Intergovernmental Panel on Climate Change.*

10. Thomas F Stocker *et al*, *Climate Change 2013: The Physical Science Basis. Working Group I Contribution to the Fifth Assessment Report of the Intergovernmental Panel on Climate Change*; Martin Parry *et al*, *Climate Change 2007: Impacts, Adaptation and Vulnerability. Contribution of Working Group II to the Fourth Assessment Report of the Intergovernmental Panel on Climate Change.*

11. Dietrich Bonhoeffer, *Letters and Papers from Prison*, enlarged edition (New York: Touchstone, 1997), 281.

Bonhoeffer, what we refer to as 'the Gandhi factor', and, in turn, those Indian natural theologies that comprise Gandhi's own influences. In developing the case for a stream of influence that reached from these Indian theologies to Bonhoeffer's tentatively emerging natural, and, specifically eco-theology, we turn first to the Gandhi factor.

Gandhi's Eco-theological Ethic

Ecology as a science examines the interrelatedness of organisms to each other and their environment. Human ecology considers the relationships between people and their environments and in particular the impact of humans on ecosystems, as well as the influence of social systems on the environment. Gandhi has been described as a human ecologist insofar as his examination of human society was not separated from where and how humans live; their organisation, ability to be productive, grow food and work were seen as taking place within the context of the natural and constructed environment and to be influenced by it.[12] His critique of industrial 'civilisation' and anticipation of environmental problems, based on over-consumption and limitless creation of 'needs', pre-empts the environmental crisis now being faced. The model Gandhi proposed for sustainable living opposed the trajectory of modern civilisation toward material welfare enhancement and profit. The model was based on a limitation of wants and the achievement of 'harmony among different elements of the social and natural order'.[13] His goal of plain living and high thinking exemplifies this approach. In what follows, one can see the connection between interrelatedness and non-violence as markers of Gandhi's eco-theology.

Gandhi's evolving worldview and personal lifestyle were influenced by both Western and Eastern thought. Whilst Gandhi's primary concern was human wellbeing, he went beyond the anthropocentric to a fundamental understanding of interrelatedness, revealing an eco-theological ethic best ascribed to Jainism, a religious influence that Gandhi openly acknowledged.[14] Whilst Gandhi was culturally

---

12. John S Moolakkattu, 'Gandhi as a Human Ecologist', in *Journal of Human Ecology* 29, no 3 (2010): 151–152.
13. 'Gandhi as a Human Ecologist', 152.
14. Michael J Nojeim, *Gandhi and King: The Power of Nonviolent Resistance* (Westport, Connecticut: Preager, 2004).

and religiously Hindu, he was attracted to the cosmology of Jainism[15] which understands *jiva* or life force to be present in all life forms, and indeed in all of creation.[16]

In Jainism, release from the cycle of rebirth is eventually attained through developing understanding of the true nature of reality, ethical practice, and commensurate purification. These are represented by 'right faith, right conduct and right knowledge'—the three 'jewels' of Jainism.[17] The Jain relationship to the environment at one level is one of deep connectivity, and this relationship is enhanced through the practices of non-violence, truthfulness, not stealing, sexual restraint and non-possession.[18] *Ahimsa*, or non-violence, became a key tenet of Gandhi's teaching regarding human interactions, dealings with the environment, and training the inner self. The Jain discipline of *ahimsa* requires that one not only remove violent behaviour from one's life, but remove also the ability to commit violence and, indeed, even the ability to conceive of it.[19] Gandhi's personal commitment to these disciplines and his ethical practice were both attractive to Bonhoeffer and, it would appear, influential, even from afar.[20]

In Jain natural theology, life and soul are present throughout all things:[21] in all moving things as well as the inanimate, *jiva* is defined according to the sense-organs possessed; where animals have five senses, the earth, air, water and vegetation have but one, that of touch.[22] Humans alone have the sixth sense of thought and thus have additional responsibility to care for and protect *jiva*.[23] 'Treading

---

15. Rajachandrea Mehta, a Jain layman, was Gandhi's guru. Jeffrey Long, 'Jainism: Key Themes', in *Religion Compass* 5, no 9 (2011): 505.
16. 'Jainism: Key Themes', 501–502; Christopher Key Chapple, 'Jainism, Ethics and Ecology', in *Bulletin for the Study of Religion* 39, no 2 (2010): 3–5.
17. Paul Dundas, Umakant Premanand Shah, and G Ralph Strohl, 'Jainism', http://www.britannica.com/EBchecked/topic/299478/Jainism/59016/Jiva-and-ajiva. Accessed 24 February 2014.
18. Agustín Pániker, *Jainism: History, Society, Philosophy and Practice* (New Delhi: Motilal Banarsidass, 2010).
19. Michael J Nojeim, *Gandhi and King: The Power of Nonviolent Resistance*.
20. See Eberhard Bethge, *Dietrich Bonhoeffer: A Biography*, Revised, illustrated edition (Minneapolis: Fortress, 2000), 105.
21. Christopher Key Chapple, 'Jainism, Ethics and Ecology', 3–4.
22. Atul N Sinha, 'Religion and Creation: Ecological Concerns in Jainism and Buddhism', *Bulletin of the Christian Institute of Religious Studies*, 27/1 (1998): 9.
23. Paul Dundas, Umakant Premanand Shah, and G Ralph Strohl, "Jainism".

lightly' on the earth, therefore, recognises and respects the sense of touch that the earth possesses. Vegetation, like humans, undergoes birth, grows, suffers, needs nourishment and dies; therefore, the *jiva* of flora must not be harmed. Jain writings warn against violating vegetation for the sake of humans or of gods. The wellbeing of the earth's vegetation is 'a symptom of [its] happiness'; the forests, 'like seers, who enduring all obstacles create welfare for all'.[24] *Ahimsa*, then, has implications for humanity's relationship not only with itself, both internally and behaviourally, but its essential relationship with the ecology.

Bonhoeffer himself describes this in the 1932 lecture, *The Right to Self-assertion*, by referring to the Upanishad phrase '*tat tvam asi*'— deriving from the refrain 'That which is the subtle essence, this whole world has for its self. That is the true. That is the self. You are that'.[25] It is a phrase denoting the oneness with the rest of existence and to which Bonhoeffer credits the Indian immersion in the natural: the 'distant, fertile, sunny form- and idea-rich world of India',[26] where:

> . . . the soul breathes the life that surrounds it in its abundance, penetrating the experience of life in the midst of this great abundance, uniting itself with it, probing and pondering its rhythm and its depths, which are basically the depths of the soul itself, and the expanses of the Indian soul are the expanses of all living things. In this way the submerging soul recognizes itself again in all that lives, as if in thousands of mirrors; out of every form of nature it hears the quiet answer: *tat tvam asi*, this is you, you yourself.[27]

According to Bonhoeffer, the Indian approach, immersed in nature, allows freedom of the soul 'for surrender and self-deepening'.[28]

---

24. Atul N Sinha, 'Religion and Creation: Ecological Concerns in Jainism and Buddhism', 9.
25. See footnote [15] in *Ecumenical, Academic, and Pastoral Work: 1931–1932*, edited by Victoria J Barnett, Mark S Brocker, and Michael B Lukens, Dietrich Bonhoeffer Works, Volume II (Minneapolis: Fortress, 2012).
26. *Ecumenical, Academic, and Pastoral Work: 1931–1932*, 250.
27. *Ecumenical, Academic, and Pastoral Work: 1931–1932*, 250.
28. *Ecumenical, Academic, and Pastoral Work: 1931–1932*, 250.

Further to the case being put, in Buddhist literature, *ahimsa* is referred to as *pranatipapt-virmana*, and conveys the same meaning. Whilst Buddhism recognises the universality of suffering within a transitory frame—hence, the life and death cycle of both flora and fauna—the Eightfold Path still demands discipline which serves to protect both the human and non-human elements of the cosmos from harm.[29] Buddhism and Jainism, both of them broadly Eastern and specifically Indian traditions emerging from a similar period, require overt behaviours commensurate with the non-violence of a disciplined mind and spirit. Gandhi, schooled in both these traditions,[30] recognised the affinity with the life and teachings of Jesus, perhaps insofar as beliefs and ethics are expressions of authentic faith, and in Jesus' commitment to non-violence. Again, in that same lecture, Bonhoeffer recognises the fundamental thread between eco-relationality and non-violence:

> And the eternal awe of the sanctity of all life comes over the soul. It aches if nature suffers violence; it is torn apart when living things are injured. You should not kill, for life is the soul, and life is you yourself; you should not do violence to any living thing; you should resist and reject anything in you that stimulates you to get your way with violence; you should tame the thirst of your passions, your hatred and your love, if they drag you to assert yourself and hurt another life. Learn to suffer, learn to go by, learn to die, all this is better than to assert oneself and to violate and live. Only in this way will your soul, which indeed is the soul of the Universe [das All] be uninjured and holy. Through love and suffering, we enter the Universe and overcome it.[31]

29. Peggy Morgan, 'Buddhism', in *Ethical Issues in Six Religious Traditions*, edited by P Morgan and CA Lawton (Edinburgh: Edinburgh University Press, 2006).
30. It is likely that Bonhoeffer also had some understanding of the Jain, Buddhist and Hindu influences on Gandhi's worldview given his deep interest in the Mahatma and his interactions with Gandhi's associates such as CF Andrews at the World Alliance. See Eberhard Bethge, *Dietrich Bonhoeffer: A Biography*, 194, 249–252.
31. Victoria J Barnett, Mark S Brocker, and Michael B Lukens, *Ecumenical, Academic, and Pastoral Work: 1931–1932*, 250–251.

Gandhi also found resonance with nineteenth century Romantics who 'romantically cherished' the pre-industrial life and the supremacy of nature.[32] An example of similar romanticism is seen in this statement:

> I need no inspiration other than Nature's. She has never failed me yet. She mystifies me, bewilders me, sends me to ecstasies.[33]

Gandhi's consideration of the environment was nonetheless more than simply romantic. He saw creation as providing the means for human survival and the provision of useful labour, whilst he urged treading lightly and bringing the 'least harm' both to other humans and to the rest of nature.[34]

Other significant Western influences on Gandhi's philosophy included Thoreau and Tolstoy.[35] Reading of Thoreau's similar experience of incarceration for civil disobedience helped kindle Gandhi's long journey of exploring and refining what *ahimsa* might mean in a political context. He coined the term *satyagraha* to describe a deeper state than mere passive resistance or civil disobedience, but rather a state of true non-violence sufficient for attaining righteous ends in a political context.

In writing on *Satyagraha and Nazism*, Gandhi advocated non-violence in the example of the situation in Czechoslovakia as a lesson for India. He continued:

> I must refuse to think that such heroism, or call it restraint, is beyond human nature. Human nature will only find itself when it fully realizes that to be human it has to cease to be beastly or brutal. Though we have the human form, without the attainment of the virtue of non-violence, we still share the qualities of our remote reputed ancestor, the orang-outang.[36]

---

32. John S Moolakkattu, 'Gandhi as a Human Ecologist', 152.
33. Cited in 'Gandhi as a Human Ecologist', 152–153.
34. 'Gandhi as a Human Ecologist', 153.
35. 'Gandhi as a Human Ecologist', 152.
36. *Harijan*, 8 October 1938, in Ronald Duncan, *Selected Writings of Mahatma Gandhi* (London: Faber & Faber, 1951), 87.

Similarly, Tolstoy's analyses of Christianity in relation to violence had an important resonance with Gandhi. Gandhi was deeply drawn to Jesus' teachings and in particular the Sermon on the Mount. Tolstoy too is drawn to the Christ but not the religion, something we return to in considering Bonhoeffer's ethic. Tolstoy examines the Sermon and finds Christianity wanting in relation to the commands against violence both in behaviour and attitude. Tolstoy systematically refutes the arguments which incrementally permit, endorse and encourage violence. He questions why it is this particular edict of Jesus which is not only disobeyed, but actively taught against by the Church. Writing just two decades before the Great War, Tolstoy could sense 'the direction in which matters were tending', and, convinced that calamity must befall Europe,[37] questioned the institutional opposition to non-violence:

> Among the many divergences of [the Church's] doctrine from the teaching of Christ, I pointed out as the chief one its omission to acknowledge the law of non-resistance to evil by violence which, more evidently than other differences, indicates how the Church doctrine prevents the teaching of Christ.[38]

To the extent that Gandhi and Tolstoy corresponded over general and specific issues around non-violence and justice, Gandhi considered himself a 'humble follower' of Tolstoy, indicating an enduring influence on the Mahatma's developing position.[39] Gandhi's social experiment in South Africa from 1910, Tolstoy Farm, was an early attempt to demonstrate *satyagraha* as a lifestyle, and was to become formational in his own political non-violence.[40] From Gandhi's view, Tolstoy Farm was based more explicitly on the articles of non-violence in Tolstoy's writings, rather than from either Hinduism or Jainism. It

---

37. Alymer Maude, 'Introduction', in *The Kingdom of God and Peace Essays*, edited (London: Geoffrey Cumberlege, Oxford University Press, 1936), xii.
38. Leo Tolstoy, 'The Kingdom of God 1893', in *The Kingdom of God and Peace Essays*, edited, *The World's Classics* (London: Geoffrey Cumberlege, Oxford University Press, 1936), 1.
39. *Mahatma Gandhi and Leo Tolstoy Letters*, edited by B Srinivasa Murthy (Long Beach: Long Beach California, 1987).
40. *Mahatma Gandhi and Leo Tolstoy Letters*, 62–78.

was also deeply committed to interfaith co-existence where religious practices across faiths were respected and shared.[41] Gandhi wrote:

> The children were saved from the infection of intolerance, and learnt to view one another's religions and customs with a large-hearted charity . . . how to live together like blood-brothers. They imbibed the lessons of mutual service, courtesy and industry . . . Even if imperfect, it was a thoughtful and religious experiment . . . [42]

Whilst it is unknown when, or to what extent Bonhoeffer was aware of the Tolstoy Farm experiment, the resonance with Bonhoeffer's own experience in communal living is noteworthy. Perhaps Bonhoeffer was mindful of Tolstoy Farm even as he experimented with communal living with the students of his confirmation class in Berlin in 1931–2.[43] Bonhoeffer's experience in the Preacher's Seminary at Zingst and then Finkewalde in 1936–7[44] was characterised by the balance of discipline and leisure, and his servant leadership was renowned. His desire and extensive preparation for communal living and shaping of ordinands found its (brief) opportunity within the oppressive political context.[45] The parallels with Gandhi's own communal experience are evident. Even Bonhoeffer's prison experiences are characterised by his desire to grasp the essence of community despite the circumstance,[46] a desire first articulated in his original thesis, *Sanctorum Communio.*[47]

Bonhoeffer and Gandhi

As Bonhoeffer's theology and work progressed, and his pacifism matured, he was increasingly drawn to the teachings emanating from the East, especially from India, and in particular from Gandhi. This interest was evoked early and in part at least by his grandmother,

---

41. *Mahatma Gandhi and Leo Tolstoy Letters.*
42. *Mahatma Gandhi and Leo Tolstoy Letters*, 71.
43. Eberhard Bethge, *Dietrich Bonhoeffer: A Biography*, 226–231.
44. *Dietrich Bonhoeffer: A Biography*, 493–586.
45. *Dietrich Bonhoeffer: A Biography*, see chapters 9 and 10.
46. *Dietrich Bonhoeffer: A Biography*, 799–934; Dietrich Bonhoeffer, *Letters and Papers from Prison.*
47. *Sanctorum Communio: A Theological Study of the Sociology of the Church*, Dietrich Bonhoeffer Works, Volume I (London: Augsberg Fortress, 1998).

who, after Bonhoeffer's year working in Spain (1928), recognised and supported his spiritual journey. She wrote:

> In your place I should try some time or other to get to know the counterpoint of the world of the east; I am thinking of India, Buddha and his world.[48]

Bonhoeffer was intent on visiting Gandhi in India and made three attempts to do so from 1929 to 1936.[49] He had a letter of introduction from C F Andrews, the Anglican missionary, friend and co-worker of Gandhi, as well as from Bishop Bell of Chichester, and a subsequent invitation from Gandhi to study with him at his ashram and travel alongside him.[50] What was the attraction?

It seems that Bonhoeffer saw in Gandhi, and the Indian natural theologies that underpinned his own eco-ethic, the authenticity for which he strove, particularly within the Confessing Church of Germany and in the network of churches with whom he was working across the West.[51] Over time, Bonhoeffer had three motivations: a desire for wider experience of the world, growing scepticism about the form Christianity was taking in the West, and searching out a legitimate form of social activism to combat Nazism. A visit to Gandhi in India would, it seems, have had potential to satisfy all three motivations.[52]

Bonhoeffer's attraction to Gandhi's 'exemplification of the Sermon on the Mount' was the duality of inner spiritual discipline coupled with social action. This aligns with the depiction of Bonhoeffer as practical mystic.[53] Bonhoeffer was seeking a 'prototype for passive resistance that could induce changes without violence'.[54] As events transpired, he chose to remain in Germany to open his alternative seminary and, as Bethge describes it: 'he would have to form his own ashram—the seminary—without prior experience in the Far East.'[55]

---

48. Eberhard Bethge, *Dietrich Bonhoeffer: A Biography*, 105.
49. *Dietrich Bonhoeffer: A Biography*, 105, 148, 407.
50. *Dietrich Bonhoeffer: A Biography*, 407.
51. *Dietrich Bonhoeffer: A Biography*.
52. *Dietrich Bonhoeffer: A Biography*, 409.
53. Terence Lovat, 'Dietrich Bonhoeffer: Interfaith Theologian and Practical Mystic', *Pacifica: Australasian Theological Studies*, 25/2 (2012).
54. Eberhard Bethge, *Dietrich Bonhoeffer: A Biography*, 409.
55. *Dietrich Bonhoeffer: A Biography*, 409.

We see parallels between Bonhoeffer's authentic spirituality and Gandhi's consistency of the inward and outward *ahimsa*. Jainism's three jewels of right faith, right knowledge and right conduct, where none is complete without the others, finds resonance in Bonhoeffer's theology (even in his first work)[56] and he later explores this desire for authenticity as part of the construct of 'religionless Christianity', whilst still situated within the limits and constraints of life: for him, this denotes the tension between the ultimate and the penultimate.[57] When he asks from his prison cell, 'Who is Christ for us today?', Bonhoeffer is, in part, exploring an authentic spirituality which pervades all aspects of life, and which, it seems, he found apparent in Gandhi. Similarly, when Bonhoeffer considers a God who would be, in Christ, 'Lord of the World',[58] he is seeking out the expression of faith which infiltrates all layers and all relationships. It is to this concept of relationships that this paper is now directed.

Bonhoeffer's Eco-theology: Creation, Suffering and Religionless Christianity

Gandhi's interest in the environment reflects his context of rural India, agri-poverty and British colonialism, where the well-being of people became his objective. Bonhoeffer's interest reflects mainly his profound Christology and the desire to see Christ's pre-eminence acknowledged and understood to underpin all of creation. The persistence and continuity of this key Christological notion throughout the Bonhoeffer corpus has been well documented.[59] Bonhoeffer's ontological understanding of humanity and creation can be seen as one of sociality rather than dominion and this is so because of the nature of the relationship between humanity and God, first glimpsed in the creation narrative (and considered by Bonhoeffer in the idea

---

56. Dietrich Bonhoeffer, *Sanctorum Communio: A Theological Study of the Sociology of the Church*.
57. *Ethics*, edited by Eberhard Bethge (New York: Touchstone, 1995), 133. Note that another key element of these questions is the historical context in which they are asked, which is beyond the scope of this paper.
58. *Letters and Papers from Prison*, 281.
59. For a review, see Kevin Lenehan, 'Reading Bonhoeffer', in *Standing Responsibly between Silence and Speech. Religion and Revelation in the Thought of Dietrich Bonhoeffer and René Girard*, edited (Leuven: Peeters, 2012), 5–33.

of participating in the 'one reality').[60] This relationship is mediated, made possible, through the work and nature of the Suffering Christ. Bonhoeffer appreciates in the Indian experience that suffering for and through nature demonstrates an intrinsic understanding of our oneness with it.[61] Reaching a position of willingness to suffer is the ultimate freedom, and this becomes possible as a manifestation of apprehending the Suffering God.[62] As Lenehan summarises it:

> We can clearly see Bonhoeffer's conviction that in Christ the interrelationality of all reality has been reconciled and restored, and that Christ is the *Mittler* [Mediator] of reality who continually makes that re-created relationality possible within reality.[63]

As the Suffering Christ is present throughout all of creation, relationship is therefore both made possible and mediated by Christ. Humanity's position in relation to non-human nature reflects the sociality possible from human to human: we acknowledge and respond to the Suffering Christ in the face of the other.[64] The God who suffers is both paradoxical and essential:

> In a world where success is the measure and justification of all things, the figure of him who was sentenced and crucified remains a stranger and is at best an object of pity...the figure of the Crucified invalidates all thought which takes success for its standard.[65]

---

60. Dietrich Bonhoeffer, *Ethics*, 195ff.
61. Victoria J Barnett, Mark S Brocker, and Michael B Lukens, *Ecumenical, Academic, and Pastoral Work: 1931–1932*, 246–257; John A Moses, *The Reluctant Revolutionary: Dietrich Bonhoeffer's Collision with Prusso-German History* (New York: Berghahn Books, 2009), 92. See Moses' full critique of 'The right to self-assertion', 90–97.
62. Dietrich Bonhoeffer, *Ethics*, 244ff.
63. Kevin Lenehan, *Standing Responsibly between Silence and Speech. Religion and Revelation in the Thought of Dietrich Bonhoeffer and René Girard*, Louvain Theological & Pastoral Monographs (Leuvan: Peeters, 2012), 522.
64. Dietrich Bonhoeffer, *Letters and Papers from Prison*, 10, 14, 370.
65. *Ethics*, 77.

For Bonhoeffer, the logical extension of the above is that we recognise the Suffering Christ in creation around us. He also explored this theme in *Creation and Fall* where he describes creation being 'subject to God in devout worship'; even the formless, mute world was already worshipping God before creatures were made.[66] Humanity's relationship with creation is now no longer 'without sin', but instead reflects the desire for domination borne of selfishness, rather than dominion of care and servanthood. In Bonhoeffer's words, 'originally man was made in the image of God, but now his likeness to God is a stolen one.'[67] Old theologies which do not move humanity toward the ultimate reconciliation and restoration[68] are artefacts and, in the context of climate crisis, a barrier to people of faith participating in the reality of the world[69] that Bonhoeffer describes.

'Stewardship' still assumes for some a preferential place for humanity, an ontological difference between human and non-human nature. What is evident in Bonhoeffer's theology, and where there is more than a measure of perceived similarity with the Eastern theologies he was investigating, is the sense of the interrelatedness of all creation, living and non-living. James Lovelock would later describe the whole of Earth as a self-regulating super-organism, *Gaia*,[70] but Bonhoeffer was more interested in how a deep Christology must be reflected in the human relationship to the rest of creation:

> The ground and animals over which I am lord constitute
> the world in which I live, without which I cease to be . . .
> I am not free from it in any sense of my essential being,
> my spirit, having no need of nature, as though nature
> were something alien to the spirit. On the contrary, in

---

66. *Creation and Fall: A Theological Exposition of Genesis 1-3*, edited by John W de Gruchy, Dietrich Bonhoeffer Works (*DBWE*) Volume 3 (Minneapolis: Fortress, 2004), 36.
67. *Ethics*, 22.
68. Rowan Williams, 'Renewing the Face of the Earth: Human Responsibility and the Environment', in *Christianity and the Renewal of Nature: Creation, Climate Change and Human Responsibility*, edited by Sebastian CH Kim and Jonathan Draper (London: SPCK, 2011), 3.
69. Dietrich Bonhoeffer, *Ethics*, 195.
70. James Lovelock, *Gaia: A New Look at Life on Earth* (Oxford: Oxford University Press, 2000).

my whole being, in my creatureliness, I belong wholly to
this world; it bears me, nurtures me, holds me.[71]

The continuity of the above with Jainism's paradigm of interconnectedness neatly characterised in the classic motif
'*Parasparopagraho Jivanam*' ('living souls render services to one
another')[72] is evident. Jainism recognises the paradox which exists.
One can, indeed must, engage in careful nurturing of the world whilst
concurrently shunning all things material. Bonhoeffer's theology
allows also for this tension: a fallen world requires care (dominion and
stewardship) whilst contemporaneously we recognise our oneness
with it, our essential relationship to it. So, in humanity's relationship
with God, we recognise a role in bringing about restoration and
reconciliation with the world. Our relationship with non-human
nature is one of servanthood:

> We do not abandon it; we do not reject it, despise it or
> condemn it, but we summon it to God, we give it hope.
> We lay hands upon it and say: God's blessing be upon
> you; may he renew you; be blessed, world created by
> God, for you belong to your creator and redeemer.[73]

Consideration of humanity's fallen relationship with the environment
demonstrates one characterised essentially by violence. Far from
the Genesis 2 fiat to 'till and keep' the garden, and appreciate it for
pleasure,[74] the relationship has been uneasy at best and damaging at
worst. At the base of humanity's behaviour toward the environment
is an attitude which does not recognise what Indian natural
theologies might call the 'life force' of non-human nature and the
interconnectedness of all life, where human life is an equal partner
and where an attitude of respect for life force, or *jiva*, underpins
action, both intentional and inadvertent. Western thought regarding

---

71. Dietrich Bonhoeffer, *Creation and Fall: A Theological Exposition of Genesis 1-3*,
    66.
72. Paul Dundas, Umakant Premanand Shah, and G Ralph Strohl, 'Jainism'.
73. Predigten II, 466 cited in *Bonhoeffer for a New Generation*, edited by Otto
    Dudzus (London: SCM, 1986), 128.
74. Gen 2:15, 9.

the environment, aided and abetted by an inadequate natural theology of dominion and stewardship, has tended toward mastery and exploitation, partly in the way controversially articulated by Lynn White.[75] In contrast, Indian natural theologies have engendered a relationship with the Earth that is much more respectful and useful to the development of an eco-theological ethic. We suggest that the discipline of non-violence which Gandhi articulated is appealing to Bonhoeffer precisely because of its consistency with the latter's inherent Christology. For him, a relationship of non-violence with non-human nature might well better reflect the meaning of 'dominion' in the creation narratives of Genesis.[76] In an allied sense, Bonhoeffer is moved to ask if our actions toward the Earth conform to the image of Christ precisely because his theology is grounded in the centrality of Christ:

> In Jesus Christ we have faith in the incarnate, crucified and risen God. In the incarnation we learn of the love of God for His creation; in the crucifixion we learn of the judgement of God upon all flesh; and in the resurrection we learn of God's will for a new world...The true significance of the world and of man is recognised precisely when it is perceived that all created things exit for the sake of Jesus Christ and consist in Him (Col 1:16ff).[77]

For Bonhoeffer, humanity's participation in the reconciliation of the world is merely a reflection of seeing the Suffering Christ in it. He describes a 'transcendence which evokes ethical responsibility' which has currency in the questions that climate change is raising for

---

75. Lynn White Jr, 'The Historical Roots of Our Ecological Crisis', in *Science* 155 (10 March 1967): 1203–1207.
76. Gen 1:26–28. Isolating the concepts of 'subdue the earth' and 'have dominion over [the other creatures]' and failing to interpret them within the literary narrative of Genesis 1–3 does not recognise the overarching theme of God's creation of a cosmos which is good, beautiful, orderly and harmonious. The role for humans over other breathing creatures is most likely to reflect God's role of dominion over all creation: that of loving care, sacrificial love and servanthood, founded upon relationship.
77. Dietrich Bonhoeffer, *Ethics*, 356.

Christian theology. He insists that we have 'no possibility of religiously concealing'[78] our responsibility for this world. That is, spirituality which is authentic is unable to hide behind traditions or dogma if they interfere with relationships which serve others. Authentic Christianity will reflect our recognition that the Suffering Christ is already in the space we seek to inhabit. In the Anthropocene, the vital relationship is that of humanity with non-human creation and that is precisely the space where Christ goes before us, actively reconciling the world to his self.[79] Bonhoeffer's eco-ethic derives from this ontology. The given relationship, whilst not equal but rightly characterised in Genesis as one of dominion, requires humanity to act with responsibility. The resultant relationship becomes one founded on love, manifesting necessarily in selflessness, rather than exploitation.

Bonhoeffer would argue that the relationship enabled through the mediation of Christ requires an attitude, and commensurate behaviour, of servanthood. How can Christ be Lord of the World if the community of believers rejects its essential task of servanthood? How can the task of reconciliation, commenced in Christ, be fulfilled in the world unless humanity participates in that very work? Christ's life and teaching demonstrate that servanthood is not dependent on being ontologically identical. Christ demonstrated both service toward, and dominion over, creation.

Behaviour toward the 'other'—non-human nature, the cosmos— via a relationship of sociality thus becomes an eco-theological ethic, driven by the interrelatedness described equivalently across faiths. Gandhi's attraction to the Jain ethic of 'treading lightly', and Bonhoeffer's relationship to the Christ in the other, derive from a truly ecological view of creation, that is, one of interrelated networks and systems of which humanity is but one part. One senses that this is moving closer to what Bonhoeffer affirms when declaring Christ to be 'Lord of the World', where 'Christ is no longer an object of religion, but something quite different',[80] and where 'religionless-secular Christians'[81] see themselves as not being 'specially favoured, but rather

78. Heinz Eduard Tödt, *Authentic Faith: Bonhoeffer's Theological Ethics in Context* (Grand Rapids: Eerdmans, 2007), 24.

79. 2 Cor 5:19; Dietrich Bonhoeffer, *Letters and Papers from Prison*, 286, 361.

80. *Letters and Papers from Prison*, 281.

81. *Letters and Papers from Prison*, 280.

as belonging wholly to the world'.[82] In the next breath, Bonhoeffer asks 'Does the secret discipline . . . take on a new importance here?'[83] in an almost identical way to that of Gandhi—where the outward behaviour characterised by non-violence is merely a manifestation of the arcane discipline.[84]

Conclusion

In searching out a Bonhoefferian eco-theological ethic that we believe can be found implicit in Bonhoeffer's Christology, we have made reference to a coincidence of thought between him and Gandhi that, evidence suggests, may amount to a veritable influence by Gandhi and his own underpinning Indian natural and eco-theologies, as well as by Western influences. In essence, the paper poses its own version of the great Bonhoefferian Christological question: 'Is this who Christ is for us today?' Is Christ throughout the cosmos, in the form of the other, demanding a sociality which requires humanity to respond to the rest of the ecology in a relationship of mutual edification rather than domination? Is this the authentic meaning of 'dominion' in a reinterpreted biblical sense? Is dominion, in the form of responsible service to the ecology, arguably Christianity's most urgent and potentially powerful expression of faith midst the current challenges of climate change? Herein, it is proposed, Bonhoeffer's inherent Christology provides in part for an eco-theology with potential to inform, enliven and embolden that expression.

---

82. *Letters and Papers from Prison*, 281.
83. *Letters and Papers from Prison*, 281.
84. *Letters and Papers from Prison*, 369.

The Bonhoeffer Society as Mentor

Keith Clements

Just what is the International Bonhoeffer Society, at any rate its English-language Section? Back in 1980, as I was leaving for my first experience of an International Bonhoeffer Congress, at Oxford, my wife wanted to know whether this was the theological equivalent of the Elvis Presley movement. A good question, though so far I don't think our Newsletter has been reporting claimed sightings of Bonhoeffer in obscure cafés or shopping malls. But it's a question which I imagine is quite seriously exercising all our minds right now, just as we are celebrating the completion of the publication of the Dietrich Bonhoeffer Works in English. (*DBWE*). For some twenty-five years, the support and promotion of this work has been a central motif of the English Language Section of the Society, and all Society members can justly claim a share in the credit for it, as well as in the general pleasure at the fulfilment of the task. For a number of those of us directly involved in the work, especially those of us from abroad, the annual meetings of the Editorial Board have been a prime reason for our coming to the American Academy of Religion and the Bonhoeffer sessions and meetings of the Society held during it. But what now, now that the *DBWE* is fully launched?

It's as well to remember that the Society in fact predates by a number of years the beginning of the *DBWE* project in the late 1980s. So some of us perhaps feel like couples who say 'Can you recall what it was like before we had the kids?' In the middle term of course parents tend to ask, 'Just why did we have the kids at all?' As a former student of mine, reflecting on the current vogue for starting up new churches of all kinds, commented: 'Conceiving is always more exciting than nurturing.' But then, when the kids have grown up and left home we ask, 'What are we here for, now? What is there left for us to do?' Or, to co-opt a question Bonhoeffer himself asked, 'Are we still of any use?'

This question has reinforced itself to me recently through two quite unexpected encounters and discoveries back in England. The first was with a student contemporary of mine at Cambridge, when last year we met at a fiftieth anniversary reunion of our college year. We had known each other in our college days, but not closely. He had studied engineering. But now it turned out that he had an enthusiasm for Bonhoeffer, so much so that he had read one of my books without realising that it was I who had written it (if you see what I mean) until our meeting up last year. In fact his enthusiasm for Bonhoeffer goes right back to his student years, when he had visited Germany and came across a book called *Widerstand und Ergebung*! It included a photograph of the author taken about 1941. He has treasured it ever since. We have now been corresponding and have met a couple of times since that reunion. In a letter of a few weeks ago he writes of sensing a kind of friendship with Bonhoeffer: '*To me the 1941 photograph is almost a photograph of a living person and he is very much alive . . . To me he has an enormous integrity in that time (which was actually during both our lifetimes even if we were very small). I have felt for much of my life scarred by the horrendous events which were occurring only a few hundred miles away. Bonhoeffer has been . . . part of a healing process.*' But the 'healing process' of which he speaks is not just that of the overall tragic history of the mid-twentieth century, but a much more personal one too. While he was a student, a tragedy occurred in his family the full facts of which were confessed to him only much later, leaving him besmirched with a sense of shared guilt. Bonhoeffer, he told me, has helped him live with those scars too.

The second is a group called 'Project Bonhoeffer' that formed in England a couple of years ago. It was initiated by people who were in the Student Christian Movement (SCM) in the early 1960s when interest in Bonhoeffer ran very high and he was very influential among more radical Christians, They now want to reignite that interest and the social concern it generated, among today's younger generation. I attended and spoke at their annual gathering in London three weeks ago and it really was an enlivening experience. At the centre of Project Bonhoeffer is a scheme whereby in association with the SCM, internships are provided for young adults to work in socially committed organisations, and to feed what they learn through that experience back into SCM as a whole – and all the time to learn something from Bonhoeffer. One of the two current interns, Victoria, a modern languages graduate, is assisting in a small but very active overseas development agency. She said Bonhoeffer had impressed her with his emphasis that it is in the world and the world of action that one meets God, the God of Christ who is the suffering, powerless, crucified one. The other, Gary, a law graduate, is placed in a group working with criminalised youth in south London. He spoke of Bonhoeffer's comment, in one of the prison letters, that to understand people you have to know what they been through and suffered.

Now neither my college friend, nor Project Bonhoeffer and its SCM interns, owe their interest and enthusiasm for Bonhoeffer in any direct way to the Bonhoeffer Society (though you'll be glad to know Project Bonhoeffer is hoping to approach the Society for some kind of affiliation). They testify to how Bonhoeffer is able to make his own appeal to people, and to impact upon their spiritual and ethical searching. To echo an old gospel hymn 'There is a fountain, deep and *wide*' of Bonhoeffer interest. So where are we in it, and what is particular about our contribution? Here is where we have to be careful. It's always tempting at times of transition and uncertainty, to rush and try to create an artificial and unnecessary peculiarity about ourselves. Sigmund Freud coined the term 'the narcissism of minor differences' to describe how individuals who are insecure or inwardly divided as to their identity, tend to exaggerate what is distinctive about themselves or even claim a kind of uniqueness. The same can apply to groups. It certainly applies to churches—as an ecumenist I'm always struck by how some churches, in the UK at least, like to claim an imagined uniqueness in some respects or even to invent distinctions to set them apart from others, even at local level. The town of Portishead where I live in England has one Anglican parish with two churches, St Nicholas and St Peter's. My wife and I since we moved to Portishead from Bristol, regularly attend St Nicholas'. After several months we were somewhat puzzled by the fact that although the church has a choir, at Sunday Eucharist we never sang, but only said, the Gloria. On asking why this was so the answer was 'Because at St Peter's they do'.

Rather than first trying to invent something apparently distinctive for us to do, let's try and identify what comes naturally to us and what we're already good at, and what we might do even better. To describe the Society I am drawn to the term 'Mentor'. In Homer's *Odyssey*, Ulysses before going off to fight the Trojan wars appoints Mentor as an adviser and counsellor for his young son Telemachus, and Mentor's name has in later ages been adopted to describe the role of one who takes under his or her wing a befriending, advisory role in the development of a less experienced person. Many of us who have been in the Bonhoeffer Society over the years will recall particular individuals who have been mentors to us, helping us to find our way in Bonhoeffer studies. Many whom we recall with gratitude and affection—even if we did not always agree with them – are no longer with us: people like Burton Nelson, Dan Hardy, John Godsey, Jim Burtness, Hans Pfeifer, Jean Bethke Elshtain. A mentor is not necessarily or formally a teacher: more often a friend, a wise and knowledgeable friend ready to talk and share his or her wisdom and experience; and just as important, to listen and to encourage by how they listen. I particularly think in this regard of that quiet, gentle figure who died sadly prematurely twenty-five years ago, Professor Gerard Rothuizen of the Netherlands. Then of course there were those, virtually all now departed, who had known Bonhoeffer well, and who especially at the International Congresses shared their memories and corrected our sometimes simplistic impressions of Bonhoeffer: former Finkenwaldians like Werner Koch, Winfried Maechler, Albrecht Schönherr. Above all, of course, Eberhard Bethge and Renate (we think of Renate now, especially in her in very advanced years and state of health). Eberhard would have laughed—loudly—at any suggestion of being a mentor, despite knowing more than any of us. He always tried, as it were, to sit to one side of Dietrich and let him do the talking, though always ready with his own comments or questions. That was itself a real mentoring because it encouraged us to pursue quite boldly our own lines of enquiry, and often Eberhard seemed to get even more excited than we ourselves at what we thought we were finding out. This could prove a rather challenging experience when being entertained at the Bethges' lunch table at their home in Rengsdorf or later at Villiprott, coping with Eberhard's questions after questions while faced with yet another helping of Renate's fruit compôte.

Such dear mentors may no longer be with us, but even in what is now its sub-apostolic age the Bonhoeffer Society is a group which can act as a corporate mentor of its members, who collectively have more wisdom than any one of us on our own. That should be inherent in the nature of a society devoted to the legacy of one who was himself a superb mentor: not just a lecturer, teacher or seminary director but a continuing friend, adviser and guide to people; and not just to his students but also for example his confirmation candidates, and individuals in his congregations in Barcelona and London—a role which has just been highlighted by the publication of *Letters to London*, Bonhoeffer's recently discovered correspondence with the young Ernst Cromwell, edited by Stephen Plant and Cromwell family members. But how well it is also conveyed by his pastoral letters to his ordinands after they had left Finkenwalde or the collective pastorates for their lonely and often perilous life in the ministry, faced with daunting ethical questions as well as personal dangers. What Bonhoeffer meant as mentor is no less conveyed in some of the letters of these former students to him, like that from Gerhard Lehne who had gone to the collective pastorate in Gross-Schlönwitz very reluctantly and with grave misgivings. Afterwards, in 1939, he writes to Bonhoeffer:

> It all turned out quite differently than I had feared. Instead of coming into the stuffy air of theological bigotry, I entered a world that united many things that I love and need: accurate theological work on the common ground of fellowship, in which one's own inabilities were never noticed in a hurtful fashion, but rather which turned work into pleasure; true fellowship under the Word that united all 'without respect to person'—and nonetheless with open-mindedness and love for everything that makes even this fallen creation worthy of love: music, literature, sports, and the beauty of the earth; a generous style of life that favourably combined the culture of old homes with the uninhibited forms of a community of young men—last, not least, a man in charge who one can indeed admire without reservation. (*DBWE* 15, 128)

The good mentor is a guide not just into academic concepts however intellectually important nor into techniques however practically useful, but into a larger conception of life and of one's own possibilities in that life. Bonhoeffer knew this because he himself had been mentored. Three important mentors of Bonhoeffer are customarily listed: his father Karl; the other Karl, Barth; and Bishop George Bell. But the list goes further. I am currently working on Bonhoeffer and the ecumenical movement, and it goes without saying that Bonhoeffer was a great ecumenist (after his own fashion, I hasten to add). But Bonhoeffer did not drop down from heaven a ready-made ecumenist. He grew step by step into that role. He was mentored into it, and by one person in particular who doesn't often appear in the spotlight: Max Diestel, superintendent of the Berlin church district which included Grunewald where Bonhoeffer's home was. Diestel in the 1920s was also secretary of the German section of the World Alliance for International Friendship through the Churches. It was he who in 1927 first spotted the potential of this bright but still very young student and suggested that he might go to Barcelona for a year as assistant pastor there. It was he who in 1930 called Bonhoeffer offering the scholarship for a year's study at Union Seminary in New York. Immediately on Bonhoeffer's return from the USA in 1931 Diestel not only encouraged him to reflect on the life-changing experiences he had had there, but convinced him he ought to go to Cambridge, England, as a youth delegate at the international conference of the World Alliance—the event which really marked Bonhoeffer's entry into ecumenical responsibility. Over ten years later, in November 1942 and in very changed circumstances for both of them, Bonhoeffer wrote a long letter to Diestel on the occasion of his seventieth birthday, full of gratitude for all that he owed to this senior friend and especially for opening him up to that wider world and ecumenical life, and for the example he had set:

> [F]or me these experiences abroad] were foundational
> for my entire life and its formation. Later I was able to be
> with you at numerous ecumenical conferences; there, just
> from your way of speaking and manoeuvring, I learned
> to recognise and understand the full responsibility of the
> German church toward other churches (*DBWE* 16, 368).

Mentoring doesn't impose itself on the one mentored. It makes itself available. It opens eyes, suggests pathways, opens up possibilities, instructs by example rather than direction, when necessary points out uncomfortable truths and realities yet finally leaves the mentored one free to make his or her own evaluation and decision. Writing to his Finkenwaldians shortly after the publication of *Discipleship* in 1937, Bonhoeffer said that while the book was dedicated in spirit to them all he did not do this on the title page 'because I did not want to claim you for my thinking and theology' (*DBWE* 15, 21). Nor, in turn, can any one of us claim to 'own' Bonhoeffer exclusively. Rather, in the Bonhoeffer Society we have a fellowship in which all can mentor and be mentored in an atmosphere of enquiry, friendship and freedom: the younger and the older; those relatively new to Bonhoeffer scholarship and those for whom it has been a long, lifetime odyssey; the specialist and the generalist; and, very importantly, the professional scholar and the non-academic who is captivated by what Bonhoeffer means for daily discipleship. Notably, the International Society as a whole provides contacts between widely contrasting contexts in which to uncover the significance of Bonhoeffer, as shown for example by the attendance at the Sigtuna Congress last year, not just from Europe and North America, but from as far afield as South Africa, Brazil, South Korea, Japan, Australia and New Zealand. And we know just how important for Bonhoeffer studies has been the work done in far-flung situations of crisis and conflict. Within the wide, global flow of Bonhoeffer interest, the Society can and should continue to offer itself as a mentor for all who wish to have their already live enthusiasm deepened, challenged and enriched. The Bonhoeffer Society, I believe, through its networking, through gatherings such as at the AAR, through its four-yearly Congresses, through its Newsletter and webpage, its openness to new and challenging perspectives from different disciplines and varied contexts, and not least through its ever-growing circle of friendships, can not only talk about Bonhoeffer but can mentor in Bonhoefferian fashion, with that "generous style of life" and continue that rich tradition of encounter, travel, shared study and convivial enjoyment of the good things of life. Even at the end of the day, Dietrich Bonhoeffer's own self-portrait was not of himself as a mentor but as the one being mentored, a *learner*. As he writes to Eberhard Bethge in that great letter of 21 July 1944, 'Later I discovered, and am still discovering, that one only *learns* to have faith by living in the full this-worldliness of life . . . I know that it is only on the path that I have finally taken that I was able to *learn* this' (DBWE 8, 486. Emphases mine). Discovering and learning: may we remain true to that perception, as we look for further ways for the Bonhoeffer Society to be mentor.

After-dinner address at the banquet of the International Bonhoeffer Society English Language Section, Zion Lutheran Church, Baltimore, 23 November 2013.

Book Reviews

Bonhoeffer the Assassin? Challenging the Myth, Recovering His Call to Peacemaking. By Mark Thiessen Nation, Anthony G Siegrist and Daniel P Umbel (Grand Rapids, Michigan: Baker Academic, 2013). ISBN 978-0-8010-3961-4. Price: US$21.77 (272 pages).

Bonhoeffer the Assassin? is certainly a title that attracts attention. What is the book about and how well is it argued?

A major focus for the book is as indicated in the title. The authors want to argue that Dietrich Bonhoeffer was not directly involved in the attempts to assassinate Hitler that culminated in the July Plot of 1944. To the contrary they see Bonhoeffer's actions during the Second World War as entirely consistent with the pacifist position that he developed during the 1930s. Apart from the historical evaluation a large part of the book is devoted to an assessment of Bonhoeffer's ethics, with the authors arguing that *Discipleship* and *Ethics* complement each other. They oppose the view that Bonhoeffer moved from a pacifist to a 'realist' position. From the perspective of the authors the analysis of Bonhoeffer's ethical development reinforces what is argued in relation to Bonhoeffer's involvement in the plot against Hitler: Bonhoeffer remained true to his pacifist position.

As a book with three authors it is relevant to indicate the contribution of each author. Mark Nation has contributed Part 1 on 'Bonhoeffer's Biography Reconsidered' and the Conclusion; his chapters focus on the issue of Bonhoeffer's alleged involvement in the assassination attempts against Hitler. Daniel Umbel and Anthony Siegrist wrote Part 2 on 'The Development of Bonhoeffer's Theological Ethics', with chapters 4 and 5 from the former, and chapters 5 and 6 from the latter. Umbel and Siegrist studied under Nation. It appears that the focus on the assassination issue derives primarily from Nation whose emphasis is more historical; however the theological analysis provided by Umbel and Siegrist is consistent with what Nation wants to establish historically. The three authors come from the Anabaptist/Mennonite tradition. This background might affect the way they approach Bonhoeffer, but the arguments they present need to be assessed on their own merits.

Two major issues need to be assessed in relation to *Bonhoeffer the Assassin?* One issue concerns the validity of the historical analysis, focusing on whether Bonhoeffer was involved in the assassination attempts against Hitler. The other issue concerns the consistency of Bonhoeffer's approach to ethics, particularly as between *Discipleship* and *Ethics*.

In relation to the first issue chapters 1 to 3 provide a succinct and competent overview of Bonhoeffer's life, giving particular attention to Bonhoeffer's involvement in the anti-Nazi struggle. Nation points out that Bonhoeffer's work for the Abweher (German military intelligence) from October 1940 until April 1943 (the time of his arrest) was motivated primarily by a desire to avoid military service. This might well be so, but the work Bonhoeffer undertook also contributed to the development of the anti-Nazi resistance. Perhaps it was not a major contribution, but the motivation was clear. Undoubtedly Bonhoeffer is portrayed in many writings as having had a close involvement in attempts to assassinate Hitler; this portrayal also contributes to the way in which Bonhoeffer is perceived in the popular imagination, giving him the aura of a hero or martyr. On closer examination, however, it is clear that Bonhoeffer's contribution was primarily in providing a theological and ethical basis for the anti-Nazi struggle. He is unlikely to have contributed significantly to the detailed political and military planning that would have been entailed; his theological work did contribute to building and sustaining the political will required if an attempt to overthrow the Nazi regime was to succeed.

Even if Bonhoeffer's involvement in the anti-Nazi plots was primarily at this general level it defies logic to believe that he would not have been aware that the assassination of Hitler and possibly other deaths might have occurred. If the change could have been achieved by peaceful methods then this undoubtedly would have been preferable. But a peaceful change was highly unlikely to occur in wartime circumstances or even if Germany had been at peace under a Nazi regime (since such a regime by definition precluded peaceful, democratic procedures for change). By being involved in the anti-Hitler plot as he was, Bonhoeffer was implicitly giving support to the use of armed force even if in as limited a form as possible. This does not mean that Bonhoeffer had abandoned his call for 'peacemaking'. However peacemaking in certain circumstances might require the use of force to remove a tyrant and to establish a peace based on foundations of justice; this is in line with justifications for tyrannicide. Eschewing the use of force altogether might simply have confirmed Hitler's hold on power; peace would have prevailed, but so would the Nazis.

What I am suggesting here is that Bonhoeffer was implicitly involved in the attempts to assassinate Hitler, irrespective of whether he took part in more detailed planning (probably not I would suggest). In terms of the argument of this book a crucial part is on pages 92–93 where Nation takes issue with Eberhard Bethge's claim that Bonhoeffer told him that 'if it fell to him to carry out the deed [of assassinating Hitler], he was prepared to do so' (as quoted, 92). Bethge obviously has some standing as Bonhoeffer's close friend and his major biographer. However Nation rejects Bethge's recollection on the grounds that his memory could have been unreliable (of course, the testimony also goes against Nation's argument). Nation develops this point further by saying that Bethge questioned Bishop George Bell's statement that Bonhoeffer had referred to Hitler as the Anti-Christ (93). It is reasonable to say that memory can be unreliable but if the recollection is corroborated through other evidence then it probably is reliable. In this case I would suggest that irrespective of the details the general point made by Bethge is valid; similarly with Bishop George Bell Bonhoeffer might not have used the term Anti-Christ but he would certainly have portrayed Hitler as a perpetrator of evil. The comment by Siegrist in one of his chapters that 'we cannot know for sure' (208) about Bonhoeffer's involvement in the assassination attempts is more measured than what appears earlier in the book.

On the second major issue that I have identified the question is whether Bonhoeffer moved from a pacifist position in *Discipleship* to a realist one in *Ethics*. Umbel and Siegrist provide a good overview of this topic in Part 2, arguing that one can make a distinction between Bonhoeffer's position in his Barcelona lecture of February 1929, and what emerged by the time of *Discipleship*, but that there is consistency then between *Discipleship* and *Ethics*. They make the point that Bonhoeffer saw the foundation of Christian ethics as lying in God's unique action, not the enunciation of moral absolutes. They see *Discipleship* as being directed primarily towards the church, whereas *Ethics* engages more with the world, but the underlying approach is the same. In relation to the overall argument of the book (and consistent with the argument in Part 1) *Discipleship* adopts a pacifist position; Umbel and Siegrist see this continuing in *Ethics*. In putting this position they take issue particularly with Larry Rasmussen who sees a shift towards realism in Bonhoeffer's later work. Another author they contend with is Jean Bethke Elshtain who cited Bonhoeffer as an example of a peacemaker who came to believe the use of force was justified in certain circumstances; this is described as a 'flawed reading' of Bonhoeffer (190).

While I believe that the book makes a good case for establishing continuity at a certain level between *Discipleship* and *Ethics*, this does not necessarily mean that Bonhoeffer was necessarily supporting pacifism in the Anabaptist/Mennonite sense by the time he was working on the latter work (coinciding with his involvement in the anti-Hitler conspiracy). Bonhoeffer remained a peacemaker but all the evidence suggests that he supported the use of force in certain extreme circumstances. I am not putting an argument in favour of Niebuhrian realism, but I think the portrayal of Reinhold Niebuhr's views in this book is a bit oversimplified (especially on pages 212–20). There is an argument for assessing whether people behave differently in collectivities as compared with relating as individuals or in small contexts. Presumably the 'love ethic' applies in all contexts, but the formulation might vary. Niebuhr can be interpreted in different ways, and his emphases can vary. Perhaps he has been used too often to justify the use of force, but the just (justifiable) war doctrine supported by Niebuhr is actually an attempt to limit the use of force. If Niebuhr has been invoked wrongly by practitioners of realpolitik that does not justify critics of Niebuhr seeing these instances as embodying the 'true' Niebuhr. A fuller, more nuanced reading of Niebuhr would be more helpful, taking account of the way in which he too can be viewed as a peacemaker. (A fuller, more nuanced reading of Bonhoeffer is also desirable given the way in which he too is invoked to support varying positions that might or might not be consistent with the 'true' Bonhoeffer.)

The book is well produced. I noticed a misspelling of Hindenburg on page 36 (not Hindenberg), and reality on page 198 (not realty).

This book is worth reading. Although I found the assessment of Bonhoeffer's involvement in the anti-Hitler conspiracy ultimately unconvincing, it was a provocative argument to engage with. The assessment of the development of Bonhoeffer's theological ethics is helpful, but does not necessarily support the position that he continued to adhere to pacifism in the wartime situation.

Derek McDougall
University of Melbourne

Die Finkenwalder Rundbriefe. **Briefe und Texte von Dietrich Bonhoeffer und seinen Predigerseminaristen 1935–1946** (Herausgegeben von Ilse Tödt, Gütersloher Verlagshaus, 2013), 709 pages.

In September 1935 Confessing Church efforts to train, ordain or install pastors in congregations and parishes were made 'illegal'. But the fraught and pressured minority church body had by then gamely established five 'preacher seminaries' for its ministerial candidates. Having completed their basic theological education elsewhere (usually at universities), these were young unmarried men who were now to deepen their learning and their practical skills before fronting up for final examinations, ordination and entry into active church service. In that very year (1935) Bonhoeffer had—along with his assistant, Pastor Wilhelm Rott—been called to start the *Predigerseminar* at Finkenwalde near the Baltic city of Stettin. Its first course began mid-year.

In prefatory remarks Ilse Tödt, chief editor of *Finkenwalder Rundbriefe*, alludes to the cooperative effort of persons in what took place on that campus and also in what has now at last led to the publication of this collection of documents in full. The legacy which reaches the present rests on the past. Which makes this is a treasure of a book in many respects. And the special contribution of Otto Berendt, last of the Finkenwaldians (see below), connects that time of seed-sowing with the now of the book on a personal level.

Almost a decade before his seminary directorship, Bonhoeffer wrote *Sanctorum Communio*, developing the key emphasis which then took on form at Finkenwalde in the community of young men engaging in daily study of the Word, discussion, worship, and in close communal life. They also engaged in outreach, in mission and preaching tours, thus coming face to face with the hard realities of secularism, nominal church membership, or hostility in nearby districts and congregations.

The quality and warmth of Christian brotherhood developing in those humble, sometimes bleak Baltic surroundings, was inspired by Bonhoeffer's vision; and by his admonition to the continuous reading of Scripture and by prayer in its various forms. He led by example, and exuded spiritual energy as well as joy and confidence. To those who went out after the first course he could write: 'The summer of 1935. . . has been the fullest time of my life, both from the professional and from the human point of view'. And: 'You have made my work easy for me' (50; English translation according to Eberhard Bethge: *Dietrich Bonhoeffer: Theologian, Christian, Contemporary* [London: Collins, 1970], 341).

At Finkenwalde Bonhoeffer and his helpers worked hard to keep in touch with their brothers. Communication, they knew, was a sine qua non for the community's survival. Twenty-three monthly circular letters to the disbursed alumni of the Finkenwalde courses/terms (there were five such) attest to this conviction. Replies from the field were sought after and warmly welcomed; resulting pertinent information was shared with all brothers in the next letter out. While Bonhoeffer authored the greater part of this correspondence, Bethge, Schönherr, Maechler and others, who stayed on to form a stabilizing bridge of brotherly continuity, joined him as authors.

After five semesters the NS closed the seminary (September 1937). Moreover, escalating Nazi harassment discouraged the further organized assembly of Confessing Church students for professional development. Bethge has described the wave of arrests at that time (*Dietrich Bonhoeffer*, 487–489). 'By the end of 1937, 804 members of the Confessing Church had been imprisoned for longer or shorter periods' (483). Yet, within months Bonhoeffer is conducting workshops and courses in so-called 'collective pastorates'—at semi-covert venues deeper into Pomerania (at Köslin, Schlawe and Gross-Schlönwitz). Visitation and communication with the Finkenwaldians now in the field is also being carried forward. Since distribution of Confessing Church material is illegal, missives to former seminarists are circulated as 'personal' letters. Eighteen of these documents have survived, all of them penned by Bonhoeffer between 1937 and Advent 1942. They fill a further 200 pages of the *Finkenwalder Rundbriefe* (though strictly they surface in the wake of that 'closed down' enterprise).

These 'personal' letters have, along with the circular letters of the first section authored by Bonhoeffer himself, been previously published in both German and English in the context of his other writing and correspondence (as it occurred in chronological sequence): in volumes 14, 15 & 16 of the *Dietrich Bonhoeffer Werke* [*Works=DBWE*]. One might be critical of now reprinting that same material in a volume billed as an *Ergänzungsband* (similar in format and supplementary to those 'definitive edition' *Works*); this consideration is, I believe, well outweighed by the virtue of presenting all materials to emerge from 'Finkenwalde' and its sequel between one set of covers. The legitimate documentary concentration of this stately volume will surely assist readers in apprehending something of the tone and standards supported by the classy, vibrant, respectful and relaxed 'brother Bonhoeffer'—only jovially did his prodigies ever refer to the 'Direktor' by his official title.

With the onset of Hitler's war many of Bonhoeffer's men of peace are called into active service. All too soon their ranks are being brutally depleted; all up, more than 70 of his 180 fledglings are cut down, almost all of them along the Eastern front! Dietrich Bonhoeffer sadly and affectionately communicates the names of the newly fallen, each a member of Christ and of the Church, clearly recalling and making mention of the particular personal and Christian qualities of every man thus called by God. Letters of solace also go to wives and parents. The scope, centre and *telos* of his *Seelsorge* in the face of deep and recurring grief can be glimpsed in the following brief though not untypical passage from one of the last of the 'personal' missives:

'Now Edgar Engler and Robert Zenke have also fallen. It is very, very sad. In their firm church stance both of these Pomeranian brothers were particularly important to the province. In every gathering one sensed how their heart belonged completely to the service of Jesus Christ and his church. They also knew themselves to be responsible in a special way for the community of brothers and served it faithfully. Uninhibited joyfulness and profound seriousness belonged to each. Those came from the same source, from faith in Jesus Christ. Now we know our brothers to be with the One whom they served here according to the divine calling. In the midst of all our sorrow let us rejoice in this' (translation as in *DBWE* 16, 240).

Similar tributes occur at pages 206–207 where three fallen Finkenwaldians are remembered; page 237 lists four brothers fallen and one missing in Russia, pages 253f mourn and celebrate a further three (including Bonhoeffer's close friend, Gerhard Vibrans) etc, etc.

But there is so much more to this tome, both of grief and hope. We learn of 'German Christian' (*DC*) authorities luring Finkenwalde candidates away from fraught and fragile minority futures into secure and 'legal' positions in the Reichskirche. Bonhoeffer is adamantly opposed to every compromise along this line. This documentation carries his repeated warnings, and his pleadings for honesty and true loyalty. But some brothers succumb. Not forgotten, those defecting are grieved over by the community and further included in the communal prayers and intercession.

Rundbriefe reveals the spiritual order of the seminary as primed to permeate and embrace the whole brotherhood. His penned advisory for candidates preparing for the pastoral office deserves continuing careful study (155–158). On campus it was simply enacted almost without resistance – in periods of silence, common worship, daily prayer and *intercession*; and in regular meditation, over the course of a week each, on particular listed passages of the Bible. These listings, also sent out in the monthly missive to those serving in congregations, are included in this volume (for example pages 62, 102, 108, 120)—an enduring facet of the Bonhoeffer legacy! This moreover is also the case with the many written meditations on texts for particular days of the church year, as penned often by Bonhoeffer, but also by various members of the community. A sentence from his 12th 'Personal Letter' makes the profoundly all important point: 'Reading the Word will ignite longing for the Word' (470).

A third, slimmer collection of documents presented in this tome reaches even further toward our time. It consists of entries written by seven members of the 'collective pastorate' run by Bonhoeffer at Sigurdshof in the summer of 1939; these pieces exist in a 'Kladde' (notebook?) and were created during the war and until October 1946, when the murder of their beloved 'Direktor' was beyond doubt. Preceded by a similar but lost document, this notebook was sent on by one participant to the next; and then it lay in limbo, overlooked for 46 years at a particular address, before being forwarded–with poignant apologies!—to the leader of the group, Eberhard Bethge. The references and reflections of the document shed light on the pressures of life during the years of Bonhoeffer's imprisonment. It also illustrates the extension of his ongoing though muted influence via his students. In his entry of 1946 Bethge, then working with Otto Dibelius, bishop of Berlin, reports on a group of 'Finkenwalder' meeting regularly for meditation and theological work based mainly on then unpublished written work of Dietrich, and then, after some 'gemuetlich' fellowship, concluding with a devotion—'just as we used to do at the seminary' (525).

Rundbriefe is thorough and definitive. The appendices list all Bonhoeffer's course participants according to their class/semester/ collective vicarage groupings between 1935 and 1939. Short biograms offer readers basic data on each of these men (some 180)—along with such for all other extra-biblical individuals mentioned throughout the work (from Albertz to Zywietz, some 490 in all!). People as famous and notable as Ebeling, Gerhard Krause and Albert Schönherr were Bonhoeffer students, along with Eugene Rose, who later worked briefly at Trinity Lutheran in Melbourne. Much of this information, now so easy of access, results from research by Danish Bonhoeffer scholar Jørgen-Glenthøj and the cooperative efforts of the German provincial churches and their archives.

Two Finkenwaldeans of great longevity—perhaps they really were the last—each played their part in having the complete 'Rundbriefe' material see the light of day. They are Bonhoeffer's close friend, confidant and biographer Eberhard Bethge; and Otto Berendts, participant in the 1936/1937 semester, Pastor and Superintendent at Reinickendorf. Both died before the project was finally realized, Bethge in 2000 aged ninety-one, Berendts in 2009 in his ninety-ninth year. Again Ilse Tödt tells the story in succinct style in her preface.

Fittingly, the editors have included Berendts' personal take on 'the Finkenwalde experiment', as he calls it (563). His 'Report of a contemporary' speaks also of life prior to and following his student years. It is a document of great interest, sobriety and maturity. This review can but underline its intrinsic importance. It is our good fortune thus to hear yet another voice from that earlier choir of noble witnesses from Finkenwalde. Surely an English translation of Berendts' enlivening account of sixty pages (533–594) will soon be required.

Maurice Schild
University of Divinity, Adelaide

The Reluctant Revolutionary: Dietrich Bonhoeffer's Collision with Prusso-German History. by John Moses. (New York & Oxford: Berghahn Books). ISBN   978-1-84545-531-6 . Price $US 120.00/£75.00 (298 pages).

The author of this book, Dr Moses is sometime Lecturer at the University of Queensland, 1965–1994; currently, he is Professorial Associate of St Mark's National Theological Institute in Canberra, Australia, an affiliated institution of Charles Sturt University.
One of Dr Moses' major theses is that Dietrich Bonhoeffer's life and thought has not been fully understood by Anglo-Saxon interpreters in as much as they have emphasised the contrasts in German history and sought explanations of the context of Bonhoeffer within these contrasts. As a historian, Dr Moses seeks to unravel the overarching continuity of German history in terms of the central importance of its 'religious dimension'. It is in this context that Dr Moses seeks understanding of Bonhoeffer as, 'a peculiarly German Lutheran kind of revolutionary.' What this means is not always easily understood, the theological grounding of Luther's theology is not as plain as the historical interests Dr Moses seeks to emphasise.
    It is Hegel's doctrine of power that is understood to be a critical factor in the developing culture of 19th century Prusso- German culture. Hegel's resolution of the tensions created by moral categories

as applicable to nations' relationships by the doctrine of, '*Machstaat*', involved postulating 'that the divine will was manifest on earth by monarchical states, and most clearly through the most powerful states . . . This is the one (which) . . . by virtue of its superior culture (and) had thereby demonstrated its intrinsic worthiness to impose itself upon its lesser neighbours. Such a state was bearer of the 'world Spirit' in Hegel's language (10–11). The educated German classes who imbibed this understanding despised and rejected Western ideas of peace and justice manifest in the Versailles settlement. Democratic principles and parliamentary democracy were alien concepts.

This understanding of German cultural developments by the German elites is identified by Moses as based on a belief in a 'Lutheran-Hegelian God who would, after the setback of a lost war in 1918, eventually bestow victory upon the German nation by allowing it to fulfil its rightful destiny' (11). (See also Moses description of Bonhoeffer's 'Doctor Vater', Reinhold Seeberg's extreme expression of these views, on page 33). This view also had implications for nature which was perceived, like the experience of German nation, as encompassing and limiting human life. Thinkers such as Nietzsche rebelled against such restriction and posited the right to self assertion through the will to power.

Moses traces Bonhoeffer's personal, academic, and family history noting the upper classes absorption of the prevailing *zeitgeist* described by Moses as *Bildungsbürgertum*, concluding that this ultra-patriotic 'Prussian solution', was widespread amongst the 'professoriate', 'especially the Protestant theologians, with very few exceptions' (31). Bonhoeffer thus was formed in this prevalent view amongst his teachers and peers and even as late as 1928 was espousing such (39–40) in Barcelona during his required vicarage before ordination.

Moses indicates Bonhoeffer's rejection of the cultural norms of his class to his academic studies in the nature of community and his view that individual freedom was only realised in relationship with others, as opposed to the will to power of the individual and the nation which was increasingly seen in the context of the rise of the Nazi movement as a threat to both individuals and Germany's relationship to other states. As opposed to the contemporary ideology Moses identifies Bonhoeffer's development of his notion of human freedom as the ability to be 'for others'. This view was grounded in his understanding that being a Christian entailed that one was called to self sacrifice. 'As a member of the Body of Christ, the church preordained that the individual was called to die after the example of Jesus of Nazareth who sacrificed himself for others' (94). Over against the imperial and individual view of self assertion Bonhoeffer asserts that true human self assertion, freedom, is to be found in the 'right to a death freely chosen'. Moses' exposition of this aspect of Bonhoeffer's thought is a deeply moving part of his presentation and provides a key to his understanding of how Bonhoeffer became a 'reluctant revolutionary'.

I don't think Moses's view of how Bonhoeffer became a 'reluctant revolutionary,' pays sufficient attention to Bonhoeffer's clear dependence upon Luther's understanding of Christian liberty expressed in his paper of November 1520 'The Freedom of a Christian' (see the exposition of the same in Jüngel's *The Freedom of a Christian: Luther's Significance for Contemporary Theology* (ET 1988).) Here Luther expounds the relationship between faith in Christ, not as a moral example, but resulting from ontological union between Christ and the believer. Luther indicates that while in Christ the believer is,

> an unworthy and condemned man, my God has given me in Christ all the riches of righteousness and salvation without any merit on my part, out of pure free mercy, so from now on I need nothing except faith which believes that this is true. Why should I not therefore freely, joyfully, with all my heart, and with an eager will do all things which I know are pleasing and acceptable to such a Father who has overwhelmed me with his inestimable riches? I will therefore give myself as a Christ to my neighbour, just as Christ offered himself to me, I will do nothing in this life except what I see is necessary, profitable, and salutary to my neighbour, since through faith I have an abundance of all good things in Christ. Martin Luther, *The Freedom of a Christian* in Selected Writings of Martin Luther. edited by TG Tappert (Philadelphia: Fortress Press, 1967.)

Rather than 'being for others' as a moral maxim based on the example of Jesus of Nazareth, Bonhoeffer understood the freedom to be for others, which becomes the touchstone of his criticism of the rising persecution of the Jews and the idolatry of Nazism, stemmed from the intimate relationship of faith between Christ the justifier and the Christian which liberates humans to be for others in the *Sanctorum Communio*. Bonhoeffer's ethics rather should be understood as having a solid orthodox Christological foundation. It is upon this foundation that he becomes what Moses indicates, a 'reluctant revolutionary'.

However, while there may be a significant weakness in Moses' interpretation of Bonhoeffer's Lutheran faith, this book is an excellent source for those interested in the historical and cultural context in which Bonhoeffer hammered out his contemporary theology which became and has become a rich source of Christian renewal in understanding discipleship in the modern world. Moses' familiarity with the German literature of the period and his grasp of the political and social issues of the times are of the highest order and is essential reading for any student wishing to understand Bonhoeffer's legacy and finds its place alongside the magisterial biographies of E Bethge and E Metaxas.

It should also be noted that Dr Moses has done much to publicise Bonhoeffer's theological and political importance not only in German history but also the contemporary culture, through academic papers and conferences *et.al.* Though this aspect of his reporting would be enhanced if he acknowledged other Australian theologians who have done and are doing excellent work in this area; an example which springs to mind would be Dr Max Champion.

WG Watson
Formerly Head of Systematic Theology
Trinity College, Brisbane

Notes for Contributors

1. Spelling

The general guide to spelling will be taken from *The Macquarie Dictionary*. We use '-ise' forms for words (and not '-ize') (so: realise, globalisation, modernise . . .). Hyphens should be used in words such as 'co-operate' and 'co-ordinate', except where the mathematical 'coordinate' is used. *The Australian Writers Dictionary* is a valuable tool for assisting with the use of hyphens. We prefer World War 1 (and not First World War). All Latin, Greek and all foreign words should be in italics and have an English translation. We prefer transliterations of biblical languages but if biblical languages are used then the English must be given in brackets. Please indicate what Greek or Hebrew font has been used.

2. Abbreviations and contractions

Abbreviations are generally not used: editor (rather than ed.), translated by (rather than trans.),, volume (rather than vol.), number (rather than no.), for example (not e.g.). Those such as USA or UN do not have full points between the letters.

Contractions, which end in the last of the whole word, should not be given a full point: Dr (Doctor), St (Saint).

3. Personal initials

Do not insert a stop or space between personal initials, as for example: AN Simple.

4. Dates and numbers

Avoid unnecessary punctuation: 24 June 1999 (and not 24 June, 1999, or June 24th , 1999). 1990s (not 1990's). Twentieth century (not 20th century). When referring to the age of a person, 'she was in her eighties', use the spelt-out form, but use figures in the hyphenated form when writing of an '80-year-old woman'. In text use of year span: 1991–8 with an en rule (not hyphen and no space) (not 1991-8), 1902–3 (and not1902-03), 1878–83. When in headings or subsections, use 1990–1992. Financial years are 1991/92. Spans of numbers: use as few digits as possible, with the exception of 11–19, where 1 is repeated. So: 112–13,103–8, 34–9, 145–53. Numbers up to ninety-nine are spelt out in the text, except where figures are needed in a string of hyphenated words (35-hour week) or where figures will assist with clarity (when several numbers are compared). Numbers over ninety-nine are usually written in numerals but can be spelt out (about a thousand people) where figures seem inappropriate in the text.

5. Hyphens and dashes

En rules (a short dash) should be used for spans of numbers: 182–3; for Christian biblical references for the verses: Mk 3:12–13; for expressions of time: May–June; expressions of distance: Adelaide–Melbourne; and where 'and' is meant. Em rules (a long dash) are used in parenthetical statements, with no gap either side. For example, 'To have wide lawns—and not any garden—is not necessary for a happy life'.

6. *Quotations*

Quotations of more than 5 lines or 30 words should be indented with an extra space above and below. Indented quotes do not have opening and closing quotation marks. Short extracts of less than 5 lines (or 30 words) may appear within the text, enclosed in single quotation marks. Quotation marks should go inside the final full point if there is any authorial comment within the sentence; that is, the full point belongs to the author as part of her/his sentence.

7. *Footnotes*

Footnotes should be used for sources you have used, published or unpublished, to a brief discussion of the sources, to develop a point out of the text, or to cross reference to other parts of the text. Footnotes, notes at the bottom of each page, or endnotes, notes at the end of each chapter, may be used in the final version when lay-out occurs.

7.1 Books:

First name (not initials) and surname, title of the book (in italics), place of publication, publisher and year (all in brackets), followed by page numbers. We do not use p or pp for footnote entries or in the text. In the text write word 'page' if necessary. In footnotes there is minimal punctuation: First reference: Victor Pfitzner, *The Islands of Peru* (Adelaide: ATF Press, 1999), 21. Second and subsequent references copy and paste name (surname only) and title of book (or abbreviated title), followed by page number. Where a title is long a suitable shorter version should be used in second and subsequent references. Pfitzner, *The Islands of Peru*, 28.

7.2 *Articles in journals:*

First name, surname, title of article, (with single inverted commas), title of the journal (in italics), volume and number, year (year in brackets), followed by a colon and then the pages of the article. We do not uses p or pp in footnotes or in the text. First reference: Victor Pfitzner, 'Where To From Here?', in *Interface: A Pyschology Review*, 1/2 (1998): 22–3.Second and subsequent references: Pfitzner, 'Where to From Here?', 38.

7.3 *Articles in books:*

First name, surname, title of article (with single inverted commas), edited by, with first name first, title of the book (in italics), place of publication, publisher and year (all in brackets), followed by a colon and then page.Victor Pfitzner, 'Yesterday, Today And Tomorrow', in *Readings in Contemporary History*, edited by Victor Pfitzner (Adelaide: ATF Press, 2002), 22–56.

7.4 *Web references*

First name, surname, title of article, web address enclosed in <...>, access date.Victor Pfitzner, 'Today and Not Tomorrow' at <www.newspoll.com. apost-au>. Accessed 20 July 2010. (No underlining).

CPSIA information can be obtained at www.ICGtesting.com
Printed in the USA
BVOW05s1839021014

369244BV00002B/6/P